It AI'nt That Hard

A Developer's Guide to Directing AI, While Pretending You Know What You're Doing

Manju Kiran R

2026

Table of Contents

Copyright

It AI'nt That Hard : *A Developer's Guide to Directing AI, While Pretending You Know What You're Doing*

9 789357 175326

ISBN: 978-93-5717-532-6

For permissions requests, contact: contact@manjukiran.com

Trademark Acknowledgements

Claude, Claude Code, Claude Opus, Claude Sonnet, and Claude Haiku are trademarks of Anthropic, PBC.

Financial Disclaimer

This book describes software development practices and processes. Nothing in this book constitutes financial, investment, or trading advice. The software application described is the author's personal project, used for illustrative purposes only. Any trading-related examples are included solely to demonstrate software engineering concepts and should not be interpreted as recommendations or strategies.

Currency and Pricing

Product features, pricing, and model names described in this book were accurate as of early 2026. Technology products evolve rapidly; refer to the respective vendors' websites for current information.

AI Assistance Disclosure

AI tools were used to review and critique drafts of this manuscript during the editing process.

Author's Note

The technical content in this book - the tools, the workflows, the costs, the code, the principles - is drawn from my actual experience building software with AI assistance. The failures are real. The costs are real. The protocols exist and I use them daily.

The narrative surrounding that content is creative non-fiction. Conversations have been reconstructed from memory and, in some cases, composed to carry arguments that emerged over weeks of scattered kitchen-table discussions into scenes that work on the page. My wife is a real developer with her own relationship to these tools, but I have taken liberties with specific dialogue, scene-setting, and the occasional anecdote to serve the narrative. Some events have been compressed, reordered, or dramatised. Some domestic details are invented because the real ones were less interesting or I simply can't remember whether it was a Tuesday or a Thursday.

Judge the principles on their merits. The stories are true in the way that matters - the lessons they carry - even where the specific words spoken are my best reconstruction rather than gospel.

A Note on Brand Names

Throughout this book, I use "the AI," "the agent," and "my AI assistant" interchangeably with specific product names. Where I name a specific product, it's because the story requires it - a product-specific feature, a pricing discussion, or a particular technical behaviour. Where I use generic terms, the lessons apply regardless of which AI coding tool you use. The principles in this book are tool-agnostic, even if my experience wasn't.

First Edition

Preface

Who This Book Is For

This book is for developers who've tried AI coding assistants and found them simultaneously impressive and infuriating.

You've seen Claude or Copilot or Cursor write a function in seconds that would have taken you twenty minutes. You've also seen them confidently produce code that breaks in production, suggest patterns you explicitly banned last sprint, and helpfully "clean up" working code into elegant wreckage.

If you've experienced both the promise and the chaos, this book is for you.

It's not a tutorial on prompt engineering. It's not a breathless manifesto about AI replacing developers. It's a practitioner's account of building real systems with AI assistance - the workflows that emerged, the failures that taught them, and the uncomfortable questions about what the job becomes when robots do the typing.

Who I Am

I've been a professional software developer for fifteen years. Most of that time was spent in iOS development, shipping apps that millions of people used, accumulating the kind of hard-won expertise that comes from debugging production issues at 3 AM while questioning your career choices.

In 2025, my wife and I started building a market analytics platform. Just two developers. Complex requirements. Tight timeline. The kind of project that would normally require a large team.

We didn't have a team. We had Claude.

What followed was a year of experimentation, failure, iteration, and eventually - something that worked. Not perfectly. But reliably. The kind of reliability you can actually build a business on.

This book documents that journey. Not the marketing version where AI magically solves everything. The real version, with the skeleton closet and the 3 AM debugging sessions and the workflows that exist because something broke badly enough to demand them.

What This Book Isn't

This book won't teach you to use any specific AI tool. The interfaces change monthly. The capabilities evolve faster than anyone can document. By the time you read this, Claude will probably have new features that make some of my workarounds obsolete.

Good. That's progress.

What won't be obsolete is the pattern: new capability creates new failure mode, which creates new process, which enables new capability. The specific tools are temporary. The meta-pattern is permanent.

This book is about the meta-pattern.

What This Book Is

It's a collection of hard-won lessons about:

- How to structure AI-assisted development so it actually scales
- Why AI agents fail in ways that are different from human failures
- What workflows, testing, documentation, and review look like when AI does the implementation
- How to maintain quality when you're not the one writing every line
- What the job becomes when "developer" shifts from "person who writes code" to "person who ensures good code gets written"

Each chapter addresses a specific problem I encountered and the solution that emerged. The solutions aren't theoretical. They're running in production. They've been tested by real deadlines with real consequences.

Some of them are probably wrong. Or at least, they'll be wrong for your context. That's fine. The value isn't in copying my exact workflows. It's in understanding the thinking that created them, so you can create your own.

The Uncomfortable Parts

I've tried to be honest about the uncomfortable aspects of AI-assisted development.

The identity questions. What does it mean to be a developer when AI does the typing? Is directing AI systems still programming? When I say "I built this," how much of the building was actually mine?

The quality questions. How do you maintain standards when you're reviewing more code than you could write? When do you trust the output, and when do you verify manually?

The economic questions. What happens to junior developers when the entry-level work gets automated? What skills matter in an oversight economy?

I don't have clean answers. I have the questions, and I have my tentative responses, and I have the suspicion that we're all figuring this out together.

How to Read This Book

The chapters are roughly chronological - the order in which I encountered problems and developed solutions. But they're also somewhat modular. If you're specifically struggling with testing, skip to Chapter 8. If documentation is your pain point, Chapter 10. If you want philosophical reflection, Chapter 17.

That said, the early chapters establish concepts that later chapters build on. Reading straight through will make more sense than random sampling.

The code examples are illustrative, not copy-paste. They're simplified versions of real implementations, designed to convey concepts rather than provide complete solutions. Your codebase isn't my codebase.

Your constraints aren't my constraints. Adapt accordingly.

The Wife

My wife appears throughout this book as a voice of perspective. She's also a developer (and hence understands the git jokes that I make). She asks obvious questions that turn out not to be obvious at all. She watches me work and notices things I've stopped noticing.

The best insights in this book often came from explaining something to someone who didn't share my assumptions.

Everyone should have someone who asks "but why?" at the right moments. If you don't have that person, consider finding one. Or become that person for someone else.

The Stakes

I wrote this book because I think we're at an inflection point.

The tools are good enough now to genuinely change how software gets built. Not in a science fiction way. In a mundane, practical, "this actually works" way.

But "good enough to change things" isn't the same as "good enough to change things well." The tools can amplify good practices or bad ones. They can enable careful development or sloppy development at scale.

They can make experts more productive or make everyone equally mediocre.

The difference is in how we use them. The workflows. The discipline. The oversight.

This book is my contribution to the "use them well" side of the ledger. Take what's useful. Discard what isn't. Build something better.

That's what developers do.

Dedication

For ***Agasthya****, who keeps*

the child in me, alive
the grown up in me, grounded
the dreamer in me, unbounded

Acknowledgements

The Inner Circle

Rekha – Every good idea in this book was either yours or got better because you challenged it. You're the one who saw that prompt engineering was just specification writing before I'd figured it out. You asked the questions I was avoiding - about over-engineering, about whether the elaborate process was necessary or just comfortable, about what the job actually is now - and you asked them while shipping your own client work with a fraction of the ceremony. You also kept our household standing, kept our son happy, and gave up more evenings together than either of us was counting so I could disappear into terminal windows and come back talking about guardrails. I owe you more than a paragraph.

Agasthya – You were 3 years old when I started this. You won't read this for years, but when you do: yes, I was typing when I should have been playing with you. I'm sorry and I will more than make it up soon. Also, you were right - the building blocks are more interesting than the code. And yes, the T-Rex will decimate the Triceratop in a fight.

Apoorva - for inspiring me to turn this potential hobby into a serious new (ad)venture. For co-inventing(?) the phrase Agentic AI Architect / Transformation Consultant with me.

aMMa (mom) , **aNNa (dad)** - For your unwavering commitment to my personal and professional success regardless of your personal circumstances. For making the hard decisions for me when I couldn't understand the long-term impact of my own well-intentioned-but-ultimately-doomed-to-fail plans.

Prasad - For standing by me, even when I haven't been able to do it myself with you. For trusting in me and pushing me when I thought I couldn't go on any longer. For being more invested in this book than I was from the very beginning. You are the reason this book exists and you will always be the pioneer of how I became an author.

Alan Waddington - You read my early drafts and told me the truth where it mattered. Every chapter is better because of your honesty.

The Tools

Anthropic and the Claude team – For building the tool that made this book both possible and necessary. The irony of writing a book about AI with AI is not lost on me.

The Ones I've Forgotten

If you helped and I didn't mention you, I owe you a coffee and an apology. The coffee is the more reliable of the two.

CHAPTER 1

Fifteen Years to Fifteen Minutes

The Demo

The demo lasted four minutes and seventeen seconds.

I know this because I watched it three times that night, and by the third viewing I'd started counting things. Keystrokes. Seconds. The number of files the AI touched. The number of times I whispered "no" at my laptop screen.

It was 11:14 PM on a Tuesday. The house was quiet in that specific way it gets after a toddler has been negotiated into sleep - the silence fragile, liable to shatter if you breathe too loud or step on that one floorboard near the bathroom. I was in my home office, which is a generous term for the corner of the spare bedroom where I keep my laptop and pretend I'm not also surrounded by nappies and a dismantled cot we've been meaning to reassemble for six months.

On screen: a developer I'd never heard of, demonstrating something called Claude Code.

"Let me build a feature," he said, with the casual confidence of someone about to ruin my evening.

He typed a prompt. Not code - a sentence. Plain English. Something about user authentication with JWT tokens and password reset functionality.

And then the AI built it.

Not suggested it. Not autocompleted a few lines. Built it. The whole thing. Files appearing like magic. Functions materialising. Tests - actual tests, not the "I'll add those later" tests we all pretend we'll add later - spinning up and passing.

Four minutes. Seventeen seconds.

I sat there, coffee going cold, and felt something I hadn't felt since my first week as a developer: genuinely lost.

To understand why this hit so hard, you need to know who was watching that demo.

The Long Road Here

I'm a civil engineer by education. Yes, really. I spent the early years of my career at one of the Big 4 consulting firms, buried in spreadsheets and stakeholder meetings, living the corporate consulting grind in all its PowerPoint-flavoured glory. Project management. Risk assessments. The sort of work where success is measured in how many people cc'd on your emails.

Then my childhood friends called with a proposition that was either brilliant or insane. "Let's start a mobile app agency."

I joined as a project manager and partner. My first year, I earned a grand total of £600.

Not a typo. Six. Hundred. Pounds. Less than my monthly coffee budget now, if we're being honest about my caffeine dependency.

But here's the thing about being the project manager at a small agency: you need to explain technical concepts to clients. Why does this feature take two weeks? What's an API? Why can't we just make it work like

Instagram? (The answer to that last one, by the way, is always "because Instagram had two hundred engineers and you have a budget of twelve thousand pounds.")

So I started learning to code. Just enough to explain things.

And then something unexpected happened. I fell in love with it.

The code wasn't just a tool for client conversations anymore. It was creative. It was logical. It was this beautiful puzzle where you could build something from nothing, and the computer would either tell you "yes, that works" or "no, you absolute muppet, that's not even close." Clear feedback. No ambiguity. No "let's circle back on that." Just right or wrong.

The project management became secondary. The coding became an obsession.

The next fifteen years were a blur. UIKit mastery, and then SwiftUI's humbling arrival. Architecture evolution: MVC to MVP to MVVM to VIPER and then back to something simpler because VIPER was, and I cannot stress this enough, completely insane. Memory management nightmares from before ARC was a thing. Auto Layout constraint systems that still give me flashbacks. Watching Steve Jobs and Tim Cook announce features I'd spend the next year implementing.

I built banking apps used by millions. Healthcare platforms that helped people manage chronic conditions. A trading application that processed real-time market data with the kind of precision that makes you very careful about decimal points.

From civil engineer to project manager to "I made six hundred quid my first year" to senior iOS developer. The journey was unconventional. But I'd earned my place. Fifteen years of accumulated wisdom, scar tissue, and strong opinions about trailing commas.

And now I was watching an AI do in four minutes what would take me a day. Maybe two, if I'm being honest.

The second viewing didn't help.

Midnight Reckoning

I'd convinced myself the first time was a trick. Edited video. Carefully rehearsed demo. The sort of thing that looks impressive until you try it yourself and discover the demo was running on a machine with specifications that don't exist in commercial reality.

So I watched again. Slower this time. Pausing. Looking for the cuts. The edits. The moment where they'd clearly spliced in pre-written code.

There weren't any.

The AI just... worked. It understood the request. It made architectural decisions - good ones, actually, the kind I'd make myself. It handled edge cases I would have caught in code review. It wrote tests that tested what tests should test, not just lines of code that happened to execute without crashing.

I felt like a craftsman watching a machine enter the factory.

That's not quite right. A craftsman watching a machine would think "well, I suppose that'll handle the boring bits." What I was watching wasn't handling the boring bits. It was handling the interesting bits. The bits I was good at. The bits I'd spent fifteen years getting good at.

My wife found me on the third viewing. She'd come to get a glass of water from the kitchen, seen the light under the office door, and done what any developer married to another developer does at midnight - come to see what was wrong with the code.

"You're making that face again," she said. Not leaning against the doorframe. Standing in it, glass of water in hand, wearing the old university hoodie she sleeps in. "The one you made after The Incident of 2017."

We don't talk about The Incident of 2017 in detail. Suffice to say it involved a production database, a Friday deployment, and the kind of phone calls that start with "So, funny story..." The lessons from that night are burned into my soul: never deploy on Friday, always check your WHERE clause, and when your wife says you're making *that* face, something has gone properly wrong.

"I think my career might be ending," I said.

She put down the water and pulled up a chair. Not the polite interest of someone humouring her husband's late-night dramatics. The focused attention of someone who speaks the same language.

"Show me."

I played the demo from the start. She watched the whole thing. Didn't interrupt. I watched her face more than the screen - I already knew every frame. Her expression went through something I recognised, because I'd been through it an hour earlier. Curiosity.

Then concentration. Then the slight tightening around the eyes that means she's doing maths she doesn't like the results of.

"Play the bit with the tests again," she said.

I scrubbed back. The AI generated the test suite. Passed everything.

"That's quite good, actually," she said.

"I know."

"Like, properly good. Not just autocomplete."

"I know."

She was quiet for a moment. Then: "The architecture choices are solid. It pulled the networking into its own layer without being told to."

"I noticed that too."

"So it's not just generating code. It's making design decisions." She leaned back in the chair. "Did you see how it handled the error states? That's not boilerplate. That's someone's - something's - opinion about error handling."

"That's the bit that got me," I said. "I could argue with the opinion. But it had one. It *had* an opinion."

"Right." She picked up her water again but didn't drink. Just held it. "My lot are still arguing about whether Copilot is worth the licence fee. This is... this is different."

"How's your React project handling it? The one with the dashboard?"

She made a face. "We're not. Tom keeps pasting suggestions from ChatGPT into Slack and calling it architecture review. Sarah's using Copilot but won't admit it in standups. Nobody's actually talking about what it means."

"What do you think it means?"

She didn't answer immediately. I appreciated that - the not answering. Too many people had instant takes. She was actually working through it.

"I think," she said slowly, "that we're going to find out the difference between what we do and what we think we do. And it might be uncomfortable."

That landed somewhere between my ribs.

"What are you going to do about it?" she asked.

I didn't have an answer. I didn't even have a coherent question yet. Just a four-minute-and-seventeen-second video playing on loop, and the growing suspicion that everything I knew about software development was about to become a historical footnote.

"Go to bed," she said, standing up. "You can panic properly in the morning."

She paused at the door. "I mean it. You're not going to solve this tonight, and you're unbearable on no sleep."

She was right. She usually is, which is one of the more exhausting aspects of being married to her. Though I suspect the exhaustion runs both ways.

I did not go to bed.

The 2 AM Scenarios

At 2 AM, I was still awake.

The bedroom was dark except for the blue glow of my phone, which I was holding at that specific angle where the light doesn't hit your partner's face and wake them up. A skill learned through many nights of being told, in no uncertain terms, to "put that thing down or go sleep on the couch."

I was reading think pieces. Hot takes. LinkedIn posts from people who definitely hadn't tried the technology but had very strong opinions about it.

"AI will replace 80% of developers within five years!"

"AI is just a toy. Real developers have nothing to worry about."

"The future belongs to prompt engineers!"

"I've tried it. It's rubbish. Can't even centre a div."

None of it helped. The optimistic takes felt like denial. The pessimistic takes felt like surrender. The balanced takes were so full of caveats they said nothing at all.

I stared at the ceiling.

What if I'd wasted fifteen years?

Not wasted in the sense of time poorly spent - I'd loved the work, mostly. Built things I was proud of. Made decent money. Had excellent arguments about tabs versus spaces with people I respected.

But wasted in the sense of... investment. Like spending years becoming an expert cartographer right before GPS was invented. All that knowledge, all that skill, all that experience - suddenly less relevant. Maybe irrelevant.

The toddler stirred beside my wife. Not awake, just that shuffling noise they make when they're fighting sleep even in their dreams. Co-sleeping: the arrangement that means I'm always one wrong move away from waking two people instead of one. I thought about him growing up in a world where "software developer" might mean something completely different than it means to me. Where the skills I'd pass on would be obsolete before he was old enough to use them.

I thought about her, too. Also a developer. Also someone who'd spent years getting good at something that might be changing underneath her. She'd been calmer about it downstairs - or at least, she'd channelled whatever she was feeling into analysis. That's her way. Mine is to spiral at 2 AM reading terrible LinkedIn takes. Hers is to go quiet, sleep on it, and come back with a framework.

I ran scenarios in my head.

Scenario one: AI is a fad. Like blockchain. Remember when everything was going to be on the blockchain? Your local curry house was going to put its loyalty card on the blockchain.

Probability: Low. The demos were too good. This wasn't vaporware.

Scenario two: AI handles the boring bits, I handle the interesting bits. We coexist. I become more productive. Life continues.

Probability: Maybe? But what if the interesting bits become the boring bits become the AI's bits?

Scenario three: Developers who adapt early become more valuable. Developers who don't become... something else. Project managers again. Consultants. The people explaining to clients why the AI-built feature took two weeks. Wait.

Probability: This felt right, actually. Uncomfortable, but right.

Scenario four: Complete obsolescence. I retrain as something the robots can't do. Plumber. Therapist. Children's party entertainer. (Actually, given the toddler's parties, that might require less adapting than I think.)

Probability: Unknown. Terrifying.

Somewhere around 3 AM, I reached a decision. Not a good decision, necessarily. Possibly a deranged decision. But a decision.

I wasn't going to ignore this. I wasn't going to dismiss it. I was going to investigate. If AI was coming for my job, I wanted to understand it well enough to either prove it couldn't take what I did, or - and this was the scary option - figure out how to use it before it used me.

By 6 AM, I'd given up on sleep entirely. Time to see what this thing could actually do.

First Contact

I installed Claude Code at 6:47 AM.

The toddler wasn't awake yet. My wife was still asleep. I had maybe forty-five minutes before the household erupted into its morning chaos of breakfast negotiations and "I don't want to wear trousers" debates.

The terminal showed a cursor. Waiting.

I typed my first prompt:

Create a SwiftUI view for a user profile screen with a circular avatar, username, and bio.

Ten seconds later, I had code.

Not good code. Functional code. The kind of code a junior developer would produce - technically correct, stylistically questionable, missing the nuance that fifteen years teaches you.

But it was code. And it had taken ten seconds.

My hands were shaking slightly. Could have been the lack of sleep. Could have been the coffee I'd stress-brewed at 5 AM. Could have been the sensation of watching the future arrive in my spare bedroom, surrounded by nappies and half-assembled baby furniture.

I tried another prompt. More complex this time. Networking layer. Error handling. The works.

More code. Better code, actually. It had paid attention to my constraints.

I tried to break it. Asked for something absurd. "Create a machine learning model that predicts user churn based on the colour of their avatar."

It politely explained why that was a terrible idea and offered alternatives. More sensible than some product managers I've worked with.

The toddler woke up. I heard him chattering to himself in his cot - the pre-cry noises that mean you have approximately four minutes before peaceful babbling becomes determined screaming.

I closed the laptop. But I was smiling.

Something had shifted. Not the fear - that was still there, would be there for a while. But now it had company.

The Seventy Percent

Here's what that morning showed me, though I didn't fully understand it until weeks later.

The AI could generate code. It was remarkably good at it. But code is maybe thirty percent of what senior developers actually do.

The other seventy percent? Let me tell you about a meeting I had three years ago.

We were eight months into a banking app rebuild. Big client, millions of users, the kind of project where a decimal point error means someone's mortgage payment goes sideways. The product manager - nice bloke, sharp on UX, maybe six months out of a bootcamp before switching to product - walked into the Thursday planning session and said, "We need offline support. Customers are complaining they can't check balances on the Tube."

Reasonable request. Simple sentence. Twelve words.

I asked seventeen questions.

Not to be difficult. Not to show off. Because fifteen years had taught me what those twelve words actually meant. Offline support for a banking app isn't caching some JSON. It's: which data can legally be stored on-device under FCA regulations? What happens when a user initiates a transfer offline and the balance has changed by the time they reconnect? How do we handle the cryptographic signing that our payment processor requires for every transaction, which needs a live handshake with their servers? What does the fraud detection team think about transactions that arrive with stale timestamps? Have we talked to compliance about storing account numbers in local SQLite, because last time someone suggested that, legal sent an email so strongly worded it practically had a restraining order attached?

The PM's face went through a journey. He'd expected "sure, two sprints." He got a whiteboard session that lasted ninety minutes and ended with a six-month roadmap and three meetings with the compliance team that none of us wanted to attend.

The code for offline caching? A week, maybe. An AI could probably rough out the CoreData schema in ten minutes. But knowing which questions to ask before writing a single line - that took fifteen years of building the wrong thing, shipping the wrong feature, sitting in the meetings where someone says "why didn't anyone think of this?"

I thought about that Thursday planning session while I made toast. The AI doesn't know about the FCA. It doesn't know our payment processor's handshake requirements. It can't read the room when the compliance officer goes quiet in a way that means you've just proposed something that will get the company fined. That knowledge lives in meeting rooms and Slack channels and those lunch conversations where the real priorities get discussed because someone let their guard down.

The AI writes code. I solve problems. Code is how problems get solved, yes. But the code is the easy part. The hard part is knowing what code to write.

That 2 AM fear - that I'd wasted fifteen years - was wrong.

Not entirely wrong. The fifteen years as I'd known them were over. The era of developers being valued primarily for typing speed and syntax knowledge - that era was ending. The tools were changing.

But the experience? The judgment? The ability to look at a solution and know it's technically correct but practically disastrous?

That was about to become more valuable, not less.

I didn't fully believe this yet. I wouldn't fully believe it for months. But standing in that kitchen at 7 AM, making toast with one hand and thinking about the demo with the other, watching my toddler cheerfully destroy a banana through methods physics shouldn't allow - I felt the beginning of a different question forming.

Not "will AI replace me?" but "how do I work with AI?"

That question would consume the next six months of my life.

The Decision

"So what's the plan?" my wife asked that evening.

The toddler was in bed. We were on the couch, her feet tucked under a cushion, her own laptop closed on the coffee table. She'd been quiet most of the day. I'd assumed she was tired. Looking back, I think she'd been doing her own version of my 2 AM spiral - just more quietly, and probably without the terrible LinkedIn posts.

"I'm going to experiment," I said. "Actually use the thing. Not tutorials. That trading project - the personal one I keep talking about and never starting."

She raised an eyebrow. "The one you've been 'about to start' for eighteen months?"

"One developer, building something that would normally take a team. If it works, I'll understand the tools properly. If it doesn't, I'll know why."

She was quiet for a moment, the way she goes quiet when she's turning something over. Not disagreeing. Not agreeing. Processing.

"That's actually not a terrible idea," she said. "Real project, real stakes. Not just a tutorial."

"High praise."

"Don't get used to it." She pulled the cushion onto her lap. "But you're going to need guardrails. You get obsessive. Remember the sourdough?"

"The sourdough was a valid culinary experiment."

"The sourdough took over the kitchen for three months and the starter is still in the back of the fridge. I'm fairly sure it's sentient by now."

"This is different."

"You say that about every obsession." But she was half-smiling. "Look, I've been thinking about it too. Since last night. That thing you showed me - it's not going to stay at that level. It's going to get better. And I don't know what that means for either of us."

There it was. Not just my crisis. Ours.

"What if we're wrong about the seventy percent?" I said. "What if judgment and experience aren't actually the hard part?"

"Then we'll deal with it. But I don't think we're wrong. Most developers don't know which bits are their actual value. They think it's the code."

"It is the code."

"It's the decisions behind the code. The code is just how the decisions get expressed." She picked up her phone, looked at it, put it down again. "Use the trading project. But set yourself a real timeframe. Don't just tinker."

"Three months?"

"Make it six. You'll underestimate everything. You always do."

"I'll try not to let it take over the spare room entirely," I said.

"Too late for that."

"I'll try not to make it worse."

"Better." She unfolded herself from the couch. "I'm going to look into it too. At work. Someone's going to have to have the conversation Tom and Sarah are avoiding. Might as well be me."

We watched something on television for a while. I don't remember what. My mind was already elsewhere - designing experiments, planning approaches, thinking about the demos I'd seen and the gaps I'd noticed and the questions nobody seemed to be asking.

How do you maintain code quality when the AI doesn't have the context of your codebase's history? How do you test AI-generated code effectively? How do you integrate this into existing workflows without creating more chaos than value?

These felt like the important questions. Not "will AI replace developers?" but "how should developers work with AI?"

The answer wasn't going to be found in LinkedIn posts or think pieces. It was going to be found in the work.

I had no idea what I was starting. But then, I hadn't known what I was starting when I left civil engineering either, and that had worked out alright.

My wife stood up, collected her phone and her laptop. "Don't stay up all night again," she said from the doorway. "You're no use to anyone running on fumes."

"I won't."

"You will." She said it without turning around. "But at least try."

I sat for a while longer in the dark, thinking about what she'd said. The decisions behind the code. Two developers in the same house, staring down the same wave. Her way of meeting it would be different from mine - steadier, probably more strategic, almost certainly less dramatic. But we were both going to have to figure it out.

The cursor would be waiting in the morning.

CHAPTER 2

My First Prompt Was Embarrassingly Bad

The Skeleton Closet

Every developer has a skeleton closet.

Some hide production databases they accidentally dropped. Others have that one regex from StackOverflow circa 2014- still don't understand it, refuse to touch it, works somehow. A few have entire repositories they've never shown another human being. Variable names like temp2_final_FINAL. Comments that just say "fix this later" from three years ago.

Mine? My first real prompt to Claude Code.

Here it is. Unedited. Preserved for posterity and public humiliation:

```
make a login screen for ios with email and
password and a button
```

Twelve words. No context. No constraints. Just vibes.

The AI equivalent of a client saying "can you make it pop?" and expecting you to know exactly what that means.

I typed that prompt at 6:52 AM, three days after the demo that started everything. My wife and son were still asleep- that precious window between "too early for any reasonable person" and "chaos begins." Maybe twenty minutes of uninterrupted time. I was going to prove this AI thing was either revolutionary or rubbish.

I hit enter.

Ten seconds later, code appeared.

```
import SwiftUI

struct LoginView: View {
  @State private var email = ""
  @State private var password = ""

  var body: some View {
    VStack {
      TextField("Email", text: $email)
      SecureField("Password", text: $password)
      Button("Login") {
        // TODO: Implement login
      }
    }
  }
}
```

A login screen. With email. And password. And a button.

Also: no styling, no validation, no accessibility labels, no keyboard handling. And a TODO where the actual functionality should be. A house with walls but no roof, no plumbing, and a note saying "add electricity later."

My first reaction was indignation. How dare this AI give me such basic code? I'd asked for a login screen, and it had given me... well, technically a login screen. But not a *good* one. Not a *real* one. Not the kind I would write.

Then I read my prompt again.

Twelve words. No mention of styling. No mention of validation. No mention of our design system, the accessibility requirements we follow, the keyboard types that should be specified. No mention that email fields should disable autocapitalisation because nobody's email starts with a capital letter except people who are wrong.

The AI had done exactly what I asked.

I was the problem. And that realisation changed everything.

The Junior Developer Moment

There's a moment in every developer's career when this realisation arrives. That junior developer you've been complaining about? They're just doing what they were told. The instructions were bad. The requirements were vague. The context was missing. And the senior developer- you, in this scenario, me in most of mine- wrote those instructions and then blamed someone else for following them.

This was that moment, except the junior developer was an AI, and there was nobody else to blame.

I thought about all the times I'd received requirements like "make the user module better" or "the checkout should be more intuitive." My personal rule that any requirement containing the word "intuitive" needed to be sent back with seventeen follow-up questions.

And here I was, writing "make a login screen for ios with email and password and a button" and expecting production-quality code.

AI isn't psychic. It's you, if you had amnesia and had just walked into the office.

Think about the last time you onboarded a new developer. You had to explain that "the API" means whichever of the seven internal APIs is currently on fire. That we never deploy on Friday because of The Incident of 2017, and no, we don't need to discuss what The Incident was, we just don't deploy on Friday, and that's final.

Claude was that new developer. Brilliant, eager, capable of working at 3 AM without complaining. But with zero institutional knowledge. Zero context about my codebase, my preferences, or the fifteen years of opinions I'd accumulated about proper software development.

When I said "login screen," I meant a polished, production-ready component with our design system, form validation, loading states, error messages, accessibility labels, and haptic feedback. I had all of that context in my head.

Claude had twelve words.

The oldest lesson in computing, and I'd managed to forget it in under a week. But at least now I knew what I was doing wrong. The question was how to do it right.

The Week of Iteration

That first prompt was a Tuesday. By Saturday, I'd learned something about Claude- and about myself.

Here's something about having a full-time job and a toddler who treats bedtime like a diplomatic negotiation with a hostile foreign power: you iterate fast or you don't iterate at all. My AI experimentation happened in stolen moments. The 6 AM window before the household erupted. The 10:30 PM hour after the third "one more story, just one more, please." When you have forty-five-minute windows, there's no room for perfectionism.

So I iterated. Same task- login screen- approached differently each day.

The second attempt, I thought the problem was length. Surely more words meant better results? I added bullet points. Email text field. Password secure field. Login button. "Nice styling."

Nice styling. Nice according to whom? The designer who still mourns skeuomorphism? The client who wants it to "look like Apple" but can't specify which era of Apple? I'd basically written "make it look professional" and expected Claude to read my mind about what professional meant.

The code that came back was styled. There was padding. The colours were blue and white. It looked like every default login screen from every tutorial ever written. Not wrong. Just generic.

By day three, I started thinking about what I actually wanted. Not in vague terms, but in specific, measurable, I-could-write-a-unit-test-for-this terms. Email TextField with keyboard type .emailAddress. Password SecureField. "Sign In" Button with blue background, white text, rounded corners. System fonts. 20pt padding. Centre everything vertically.

Now we were getting somewhere. I'd started writing prompts the way I wished clients would write user stories. The way I'd begged project managers to write requirements for fifteen years, usually while they looked at me like I was being unnecessarily difficult.

Specific. Measurable. Not open to interpretation on a Monday morning before coffee.

Every time I'd sent a requirements document back with "what do you mean by 'intuitive'?"- I was training for this moment. All those frustrating conversations about unclear specifications had prepared me to write clear prompts. The code that came back was usable. Not perfect, but a starting point, not a punchline.

But I wasn't done learning yet. Day four brought a different lesson entirely.

The Power of Negation

I spent forty precious toddler-is-asleep minutes fighting with Claude about why it kept adding authentication logic to my UI component.

I wanted a view. Just the visual layer. The networking and authentication would live elsewhere- in a view model, a service, somewhere that wasn't the UI. But Claude kept adding login functions, API calls, error handling, the works.

Then it hit me. Claude wasn't being difficult. It was being *helpful.* Login screens usually need authentication. Claude was trying to give me what it thought I needed, not what I'd asked for.

I wasn't wrong. Claude wasn't wrong. We were just operating with different assumptions.

That's when I discovered the power of negation. I started adding what I *didn't* want. Create only the LoginView UI component. Do NOT implement any authentication logic. Do NOT add any networking code.

Do NOT create a view model. Just the view. The UI. Nothing else.

Beautiful. Clean. Exactly what I asked for.

Telling Claude what to leave alone was as important as telling it what to build. It's the difference between "buy groceries" and "buy groceries for Saturday's dinner party- we're having Italian, one guest is gluten-free, and don't get the expensive olive oil because I'm not paying twelve pounds for marketing." Same task. Very different shopping trolley.

By day six, my prompts had evolved into something I barely recognised. Twelve words had become two hundred. Zero context had become full context - project details, architecture decisions, explicit requirements, and a whole section dedicated to what I *didn't* want.

Context about the project- fintech app, Combine for reactive programming, authentication goes through an existing AuthService. Architecture requirements for the ViewModel. View requirements down to the keyboard type and autocapitalisation settings. And crucially, a "Not In Scope" section listing everything Claude should keep its helpful hands off of.

This prompt produced code I could actually use. Not toy code. Not tutorial code. Production-adjacent code that needed twenty minutes of polish rather than a complete rewrite.

Six days. From "make a login screen" to genuinely useful output. Not because the AI got smarter- because I learned how to talk to it.

Requirements Engineering by Another Name

My wife had been watching the evolution all week.

Not in a looking-over-my-shoulder kind of way. She'd been at the kitchen table most evenings with her own laptop, working through a client's API integration while I ran my prompt experiments two seats away. The toddler's bedtime had become the starting gun for our parallel work sessions- two developers, one kitchen table, the lingering smell of whatever we'd heated up for dinner. On Wednesday she'd asked why I was doing the same login screen for the third time. I'd explained the iteration. She'd nodded and gone back to her own work.

By Saturday she had opinions.

"You're basically writing requirements documents," she said, closing her own laptop and stretching. "For a robot."

"It's prompt engineering," I said, with the defensive tone of someone who knows they're about to lose an argument.

"It's requirements engineering. Same thing you've been doing for fifteen years, just with a different audience." She pulled my laptop towards her and scrolled through my prompt history. "Actually, your day-six prompt is better than most of the specs you send me to review."

"Thanks. I think."

"I'm serious. You've never once written a JIRA ticket this clearly."

"JIRA tickets don't hallucinate if you're vague."

"Don't they? You've seen what the offshore team builds from vague tickets. At least Claude doesn't add twelve unrelated features and call it initiative."

The offshore team comparison was uncomfortably accurate. But something else was nagging at me.

"Have you tried it?" I asked. "Claude, I mean. For your stuff."

"Thursday night, after you went to bed." She said it casually, like she hadn't been sitting on this for two days. "I gave it a data migration spec I'd been putting off. Thirty lines of requirements. Schema changes, migration script, rollback procedures- all generated."

"Thirty lines. Your first prompt was thirty lines?"

"I write clear requirements for a living, Manju."

She wasn't gloating. "How is this different from writing a spec? You've written specs. You know what a good brief looks like." Her client work had always been spec-heavy- careful acceptance criteria, explicit edge cases, the methodical approach that made me look like a cowboy by comparison. She wasn't claiming some innate superiority. She was pointing out that the skill already existed and I'd somehow failed to recognise it in a new context.

"So you just... wrote a good prompt. First try."

"Not first try. But I didn't start with twelve words, either." She reached for her tea, found it cold, made a face. "I started the way I start any spec. Who's the audience, what do they know, what do they need, what should they not touch. The audience just happened to be an AI instead of a contractor in Hyderabad."

I sat with that for a moment. The template I'd arrived at by week's end wasn't revolutionary:

Task: one sentence describing what you want.

Context: project details, architecture patterns, relevant constraints.

Requirements: specific, measurable, as many as needed.

Constraints: technical and style boundaries.

Example: show, don't tell. Not In Scope: what you don't want.

That last section was the breakthrough. AI wants to help. Sometimes helping means adding things you didn't ask for- like the colleague who "improves" your pull request with unrelated refactoring, turning a one-line change into a three-hundred-line diff.

"The 'Not In Scope' section, though," she said. "That's the bit that matters. The rest is just good communication. The negation is the new thing."

"How did your migration go?"

"Ninety percent there. One foreign key reference wrong, rollback order needed adjusting. Twenty minutes of cleanup instead of half a day writing it from scratch." She paused. "It's a bit unsettling, honestly. Not the quality- the quality's what I'd expect from clear requirements. But getting a half-day task back in thirty seconds makes you wonder what the rest of your day is supposed to look like."

That was the first time either of us had said it out loud. Not the big existential dread from Chapter 1. Something quieter. The small, practical vertigo of a Tuesday evening becoming unexpectedly free.

She picked up her cold tea, decided to drink it anyway, and pulled the template towards her again.

"Context: I've had a long day," she said. "Requirements: you make dinner. Constraints: nothing that requires more than twenty minutes. Not In Scope: asking me to help."

"That's the second-best prompt I've heard all week."

"What's the first?"

"The thirty-line migration spec. Obviously."

She laughed. Reopened her laptop. I reopened mine. Two developers, kitchen table, Saturday night. The toddler monitor glowing green on the counter between us.

But there was a deeper lesson underneath all this structure- one that took me longer to articulate.

The Clarity Tax

Here's the uncomfortable truth I had to confront during that week: writing good prompts requires knowing what you actually want. Specifically. Precisely. Unambiguously.

If you can't write a clear prompt, you probably don't know what you want yet. And that's valuable information- it means you need to think more before you type more. The prompt isn't the starting point. The clarity is.

Scrolling back through that first week's command history, the evolution was embarrassing to witness. Twelve words to two hundred. Vague to specific. Hopeful to precise.

We've spent years complaining about unclear client requirements. "The specification is too vague." "Why can't they just tell us what they need?"

We just didn't expect to become our own unclear clients.

The gap between a bad prompt and a good prompt is the gap between code you throw away and code you ship. It's also why some developers conclude "AI can't do real work"- they tried once, got garbage, and gave up.

AI can do real work. You just have to learn to speak its language. And its language, it turns out, is the same language we've been trying to teach clients for years. Clarity. Specificity. Context. Constraints.

My wife had reached this conclusion faster. Not because she's smarter- though she'd dispute that framing- but because her workflow was already built around writing unambiguous specifications for people who didn't share her context. Years on distributed teams where a vague requirement meant a wasted sprint across three time zones. She'd been prompt engineering before prompts were a thing.

Six days for me. One evening for her. Because she'd never dressed it up as anything other than what it was:

clear communication with someone who doesn't know what you know.

The Prompt in the History

That twelve-word prompt still exists in my command history somewhere. I keep it there the same way I keep a screenshot of a code review from my first year- the one that said "this is not how professionals write code" and then explained, in detail, exactly why.

Humbling. Necessary.

My prompts look nothing like that first one now. They're structured. Specific. They tell the AI what I want, what I don't want, and why any of it matters. But I wouldn't have gotten here without starting there.

I chose to learn. Partly because I could feel the potential underneath the frustration. And partly because of that Saturday evening at the kitchen table- watching my wife get a clean migration script from her first real attempt while I'd spent a week learning to write a login screen prompt that didn't produce rubbish. The skill had been sitting in both of us all along, hiding inside fifteen years of requirements documents and client specifications. She'd recognised it faster, because she'd never stopped thinking of clear communication as the job.

I'd convinced myself the job was the code. It never was. The job was knowing what to ask for.

CHAPTER 3

The Dream That Died at 3 AM

The Vision

I had a dream.

Not the Martin Luther King kind. The dangerous kind - the kind that makes you text yourself at midnight so you don't forget it.

Picture this: It's 6 AM. I'm asleep. The toddler is asleep. The house is quiet in that fragile way that means nobody has woken up demanding dinosaur videos yet. And somewhere in the corner of my office, my machine is not asleep. My machine is working.

A daemon I've written polls GitHub every thirty seconds. A new PR appears. The daemon springs to action, spawns a Claude session, and Claude reviews the pull request - checks the code, validates against acceptance criteria, runs tests, leaves detailed comments. By the time I check my phone over breakfast, there's a notification waiting: "PR #127 reviewed. 2 comments. Ready for merge."

All while I dreamed of electric sheep.

But wait. The dream was bigger than that.

What if the PR had issues? In my grand vision, the review bot wouldn't just comment. It would talk to the implementing agent. A conversation between AI systems, happening in git-ignored threads while I remained blissfully unconscious. "Hey, you missed edge case X." The implementing agent fixes, pushes, requests re-review. The reviewer checks again. Review-fix-review-approve. AI agents resolving their differences like mature adults while I slept.

Automated. Continuous. Self-healing.

I spent four days building this system. Then I discovered it was architecturally impossible.

Let me walk you through my reasoning, because honestly, it was sound. That's the frustrating part.

The Architecture That Made Perfect Sense

The logic was impeccable. The execution was professional. The entire foundation was rotten.

The architecture had three components. First, a PR monitor written in Node.js - clean code, environment variables, proper logging. I even added graceful shutdown handlers because my first software mentor once told me that gracefulness matters, in both developers and their products. I remembered that lesson. I forgot some other, more important ones.

```
const config = {
  repos: [
    'myorg/backend-api',
    'myorg/data-services',
    'myorg/frontend-app'
  ],
  pollInterval: 30000,
  claudePath: '/usr/local/bin/claude'
};
```

It looked professional. It felt professional. Like a real system built by a real engineer who knew what he was doing.

Second component: a trigger script that would invoke Claude with a command. Just a shell script. Nothing fancy.

```
claude - command "/pr-review ${PR_URL}"
```

Third component: my /pr-review command, which was already mature at this point. Fetch PR details, create an isolated workspace, run local git diffs, validate against acceptance criteria, leave review comments. All the pieces existed. I just needed to connect them.

Like Lego. What could go wrong?

GitHub webhook or polling detects PR. Spawn Claude Code session. Execute the review command. Post results. Loop. Simple. Clean.

Wrong.

Day one was foundations. I built the Node.js service with the care of someone constructing a cathedral. The monitoring worked. The polling worked.

Everything worked, right up until the part where it needed to actually talk to Claude.

Day two was when I should have stopped.

The Integration That Wouldn't

My first attempt at Claude integration was direct CLI invocation. Just call Claude with a command, like any other tool. Problem: Claude starts an interactive session. It expects human input. It sits there, waiting, cursor blinking, while my daemon stares at it and nothing happens.

Second attempt: environment variables. Maybe Claude would read a command from an env var? Problem: that's not how Claude works. I was guessing at interfaces that didn't exist.

Third attempt: heredoc input. Pipe the command into Claude's standard input.

```
claude << EOF
/pr-review https://github.com/myorg/backend-
api/pull/42
EOF
```

Problem: Claude's session model doesn't accept piped input to commands. The characters went in. Nothing came out. Like shouting into a pillow.

My wife was on the sofa that evening with her own laptop - she'd been debugging a CSS specificity nightmare on one of her projects all afternoon. She'd glanced over a few times as I cycled through terminal windows, eight of them, maybe nine, each representing a different failed approach.

"What are you actually trying to get it to do?" she asked, not looking up from her screen.

"Automated PR reviews. The monitor detects a new PR, spawns a Claude session, runs the review command, posts comments. All while I sleep."

"And the spawning bit is the problem."

"The invocation, yeah. I can't find the right way to pass it a command non-interactively."

She closed her laptop lid halfway and studied my terminal windows. "Have you actually tried piping a command to it? Just the basic thing. One terminal, one pipe."

"I'm building the orchestration layer first - the polling, the triggers, the error handling. Once that's solid I'll wire up the Claude integration."

"Manju." She pulled up a terminal of her own. "Last month I spent two days building a caching layer for an API that turned out to have a rate limit of ten requests per hour. Beautiful Redis setup. Completely pointless, because I never checked the constraint that mattered."

"This is different. The architecture is sound."

"The architecture is the top four floors of a building. I'm asking about the foundation."

"I will. After I finish the trigger script."

She looked at me for a long moment - not annoyed, but with the weariness of someone watching a mistake they recognise from the inside. She'd made this class of error before. She could see the shape of it.

"Right," she said. "Crack on, then."

She went back to her CSS. I went back to my trigger script. We both knew how this was going to end.

The Desperation Phase

Maybe I was approaching this wrong. What if I could run Claude in a persistent session and send commands through IPC? What if there was some headless mode I hadn't discovered, lurking in the documentation like an Easter egg?

I tried screen sessions:

```
screen -dmS claude_review "claude"
screen -S claude_review -X stuff "/pr-review
${URL}^M"
```

I tried expect scripts:

```
spawn claude
expect ">"
send "/pr-review $url\r"
```

I tried things I'm not proud of. Things that belong next to that twelve-word prompt from Chapter 2 and the regex I still don't understand from 2014.

Nothing worked.

At some point around midnight, I asked Claude itself how to automate Claude. The irony was not lost on me. It gave me thoughtful suggestions that didn't work, which felt appropriate somehow. Even the AI couldn't figure out how to automate itself.

The coffee had stopped helping hours ago but I kept drinking it anyway, because admitting the coffee wasn't helping meant admitting I should go to bed, and admitting I should go to bed meant admitting this wasn't going to work, and I wasn't ready to admit that yet.

By 3 AM, I had no choice.

Acceptance

Day four. 3 AM.

I was surrounded by terminal windows. Empty coffee cups formed a small city on my desk. The specific delirium that comes from debugging something you're slowly realising is impossible had settled over me like a fog.

I accepted the truth.

Claude Code is designed for interactive sessions with humans. Not for programmatic invocation. Not for piped commands. Not for daemons that spawn it at 6 AM while developers sleep.

The dream was dead.

I sat there for a while, staring at the code I'd written. Good code. Clean code. Useless code. Four days of careful engineering that would never run in production because the fundamental assumption - that Claude could accept commands from a script - was wrong.

It's a particular kind of defeat, building something that works perfectly except for the one thing it needs to do. Like constructing a beautiful car and then discovering you forgot to include an engine.

Fifteen minutes. That's how long it would have taken to discover this didn't work. Open a terminal. Try to pipe a command to Claude. Watch it fail. Move on with my life. I knew this. On some level, I knew this the whole time.

Instead: four days. Because the architecture was seductive. Three clean components, a mermaid diagram that looked like it belonged in a systems design textbook, graceful shutdown handlers. When the design is beautiful enough, you stop questioning whether it stands on anything.

My wife had asked the right question on Day 2 - "Have you actually tried piping a command to it?" - and I'd brushed past it because I was in love with the architecture. Every experienced developer has done this. Built the cathedral before testing the soil. I'd spent fifteen years warning clients about exactly this pattern, and I'd walked straight into it because the vision was too pretty to question.

You can't pipe into a conversation. Conversations require conversants. It's like trying to automate a Socratic dialogue. The whole point is the back-and-forth. Take away the back-and-forth and you don't have a more efficient dialogue - you have nothing.

Maybe by the time you read this, my dream is possible. Check your Claude version. If headless mode is there, pour one out for past me.

I told her over breakfast. She was feeding the toddler, who was distributing porridge across surfaces in ways that suggested a future in abstract expressionism.

"The pipe doesn't work," I said. "Interactive sessions only. The whole thing is dead."

She didn't say I told you so. What she said was worse, in a way, because it was generous.

"The review command itself - that works, though? The bit where you actually run the review?"

"Yeah. That part's solid."

"So you built a good review tool and a dead automation layer. Keep the good bit. Bin the dead bit." She wiped porridge off the table. "You've got a command that does a ninety-second review. That's not nothing, Manju. That's actually useful."

The kindness stung more than smugness would have. We'd both made the same class of mistake before - build first, validate later. She'd learned to check the foundations earlier than I had on this particular project. Next time, I'd check first. The expensive lesson was, at least, a permanent one.

Every workflow I built after that night - dev-workflow, child-ticket-workflow, pr-merge, all of them - started with a question that now lives in my bones: does the basic thing work? Not the elegant thing. Not the automated thing. The basic thing. The fifteen-minute test that either lets you build with confidence or saves you four days of cathedral construction on sand.

The dream of automated reviews while sleeping died at 3 AM on a Thursday. What took its place was a manual-but-fast review command. One line in the terminal:

```
/pr-review https://github.com/myorg/backend-
api/pull/42
```

Ninety seconds later, a thorough review. Not automatic. But fast enough that "manual" doesn't hurt. The first time I ran it and watched a review appear before my toast popped, I felt something I hadn't expected - not the triumph of the dream, but the quieter satisfaction of a thing that actually works.

I saved the dead code to a folder called pr-review-bots - deprecated, because I couldn't quite bring myself to delete it. Architects rarely can.

CHAPTER 4

Setting Up the Orchestra Pit

The Invisible Foundation

Nobody applauds the orchestra pit.

The symphony ends. Standing ovation. The conductor bows with practised humility. The first violinist takes her moment in the spotlight. And beneath the stage, invisible, sits the pit: risers calibrated to the inch, acoustic panels angled for optimal resonance, cable management that prevents a trombone from murdering the first chair with a stray power cord.

Without the pit, no performance. But nobody thinks about the pit. They think about the music.

AI-assisted development has its own orchestra pit. Directory structures. Configuration files. The documentation that tells Claude where things live and how we broke them last time. Unsexy work. The kind that separates a cool demo from a system that survives contact with production.

This chapter is about plumbing. Configuration files. Directory structures. The pre-commit hook, which checks your work before you're allowed to submit it, like a bouncer at a nightclub except the nightclub is a code repository and the dress code is "must pass type checking." This is also the infrastructure that makes everything else in this book possible. The prompts from Chapter 2 were the sheet music. This chapter is the pit that lets the orchestra play it.

The first problem I had to solve was fundamental: Claude's memory, or rather, the complete absence of it.

The Amnesia Problem

Close a Claude session. Start a new one. Claude remembers nothing.

No codebase. No architecture decisions. No memory of that brilliant workaround you implemented at 2 AM because the API returned snake_case on Tuesdays and camelCase the rest of the week, and you still don't know why, and you've stopped asking because some mysteries are better left unsolved.

Every session starts at zero. It's like onboarding a new developer, except this one shows up every single morning asking where the toilets are. Brilliant, capable, eager to help - and completely without context about anything that happened before they walked through the door.

There's something quietly strange about that, if you sit with it. You work closely with this thing for hours. You develop a rhythm, a shorthand. It starts to feel like collaboration. Then you close the session, open a new one, and it has no idea who you are. Every session is a first date. You bring the entire history of the relationship; it brings nothing. The CLAUDE.md file I'm about to describe is, in a way, a letter you write to someone who will never remember receiving the last one.

This isn't a bug. It's how the technology works. But it means that if we want Claude to be useful beyond trivial one-off tasks, we need to give it context another way. We need to write down everything a new team member would need to know, and make sure Claude reads it before doing anything else.

Enter ***CLAUDE.md.***

The name is straightforward: a markdown file that Claude reads automatically when it starts working on a project. Your chance to say everything you wish you'd told that contractor before they "refactored" your authentication module into something that technically worked but made everyone who looked at it feel vaguely unwell.

My first CLAUDE.md was three lines. Project name. Tech stack. "Don't use mock data." It helped, marginally. Like writing "good luck" on a napkin and calling it a briefing.

By month two, it had grown to five hundred lines. Every decision. Every gotcha. Every time something had broken and why. It was comprehensive, thorough, and completely counterproductive - Claude read the entire thing at the start of every session, burning tokens and time on context that might not be relevant to the task at hand. Like handing someone the entire Encyclopaedia Britannica when they asked for directions to the kitchen.

The breakthrough came when I started thinking about newspapers. Important stuff at the top. Details below. Extended content behind links for readers who want depth. Claude could follow links when it needed more information, but the core context stayed scannable.

Project overview: what this thing is, who it's for, why it exists. Directory structure: where things live, named simply so there's no ambiguity. Tech stack: versions matter, because the difference between Python 3.9 and 3.11 isn't academic when async breaks. Code conventions: absolute imports, existing patterns, tests required. And crucially, how to run the checks locally, because we don't pay for cloud CI and Claude needs to know that.

This file became my handshake with Claude. Here's what you're working with. Here's how we do things. Here's where the bodies are buried.

But one file wasn't enough. Context needed to cascade.

Context Feng Shui

It was a Saturday afternoon. My wife was at the kitchen table with her laptop, refactoring a component library for one of her clients. I was at the desk in the next room, staring at a CLAUDE.md that had outgrown its usefulness for the third time that month. Every time I opened a frontend session, Claude loaded five hundred lines about backend database migrations. Every backend session started with React component conventions it would never touch.

The answer was obvious, once I stopped trying to fit everything into one file: layers. A global file with preferences that apply everywhere. A project-level file with specifics for this codebase. Directory-level files for backend versus frontend. Module-level files for the tricky corners. Broad to narrow, general to specific, each layer only adding what's relevant to its scope.

"I'm cascading the CLAUDE.md files," I told my wife through the doorway. "Global at the top, project overrides global, directory overrides project. Most specific wins."

She stopped typing. "Like CSS specificity."

"Exactly. Or building codes - national rules set the baseline, state rules narrow them, city codes get specific."

"I was going to say CSS but building codes works too." She went back to her component library. "Are you putting the global one in the project root?"

"No - home directory. Above any individual project, so it applies to everything I work on."

"That makes sense. Mine would go in the project root since I'm only using it for one client at a time, but if you've got multiple projects, yeah. Home directory."

Good architectural thinking still needs to be adapted to the actual constraints of the system. The cascade pattern was clear. The placement depended on how many projects you're juggling.

The structure I built looked like this. At the top level, in my home directory, sits a global CLAUDE.md. The preferences that apply everywhere: I use Linear for tickets. British spelling, always. Never deploy on Fridays, and we don't need to discuss why. These are the rules for every project I touch, the baseline that Claude should know regardless of what codebase we're working in.

At the project root sits another CLAUDE.md. This one describes the specific project: fintech dashboard, React frontend, FastAPI backend.

Inside the backend directory, another CLAUDE.md. SQLAlchemy 2.0 patterns. Alembic for migrations - and yes, you actually need to run them, Claude, that's not optional. Pydantic v2 for validation. The specifics that apply to backend work but not to frontend work.

And in particularly complex areas - authentication, payments, anything that's been refactored more than twice - another CLAUDE.md with the accumulated wisdom of everyone who's touched that code and lived to tell the tale.

When Claude works in the authentication module, it sees all four levels:

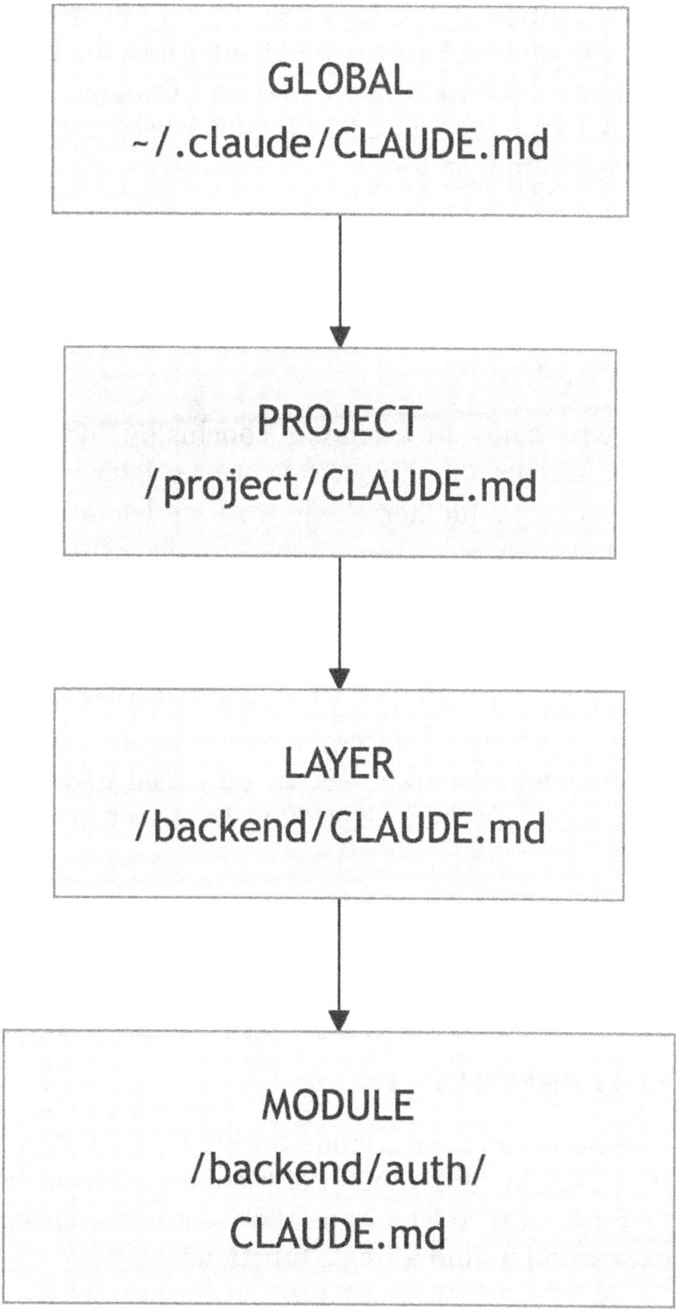
GLOBAL
~/.claude/CLAUDE.md
PROJECT
/project/CLAUDE.md
LAYER
/backend/CLAUDE.md
MODULE
/backend/auth/
CLAUDE.md

Global preferences cascade down. Project context inherits global. Layer context inherits project. Module context inherits layer. When Claude works in /backend/auth/, it sees all four levels. Everything it needs, nothing it doesn't.

No more making the plumber read the electrical blueprints before fixing the sink. Each session gets only what it needs. Frontend work sees frontend context. Backend sees backend. The right information at the right level.

My wife came to a similar conclusion independently with her own tooling a few weeks later. She'd been using Cursor for her client work and found the same bloat problem - too much context drowning the relevant bits. She didn't use a four-tier cascade; she used two tiers, because her projects were smaller and didn't need the granularity. Different problem, same principle. I mention this because there's a temptation, when you find a pattern that works, to assume your specific implementation is the universal answer. It isn't. The cascade is the insight. Four levels is just my version of it.

The context was organised. Now the code needed to be.

Boring Infrastructure, Essential Infrastructure

Directory structure sounds boring because it is boring. It's also the difference between a codebase you can navigate at 3 AM and one that requires archaeological excavation to find a single function.

The principle is predictable patterns. Components always means UI elements. Services always means business logic. Models always means data structures. Every codebase has a utils folder, and every developer who's been at this long enough has opinions about theirs. Mine started as the place for functions that didn't fit anywhere else, and honestly, it still is - but at least they're all in one place instead of scattered across the codebase like confetti.

When Claude encounters a new codebase following these patterns, it can navigate by convention. It doesn't need to ask where the API endpoints live or where the database models are defined. They're where they should be. Boring. Predictable. Essential.

The documentation lives near the code, in a docs directory that's actually maintained because Claude reads it and uses it. Architecture decisions in docs/architecture. API specifications in docs/api-specs. Decision records - those markdown files explaining why we chose Postgres over MongoDB, why we use JWT with refresh tokens, why the payments service has three different retry strategies - in docs/decisions.

That last point deserves a pause, because it describes something I'd been chasing for years. Documentation that gets used is documentation that gets maintained, which is documentation that stays accurate - a cycle that actually sustains itself. Every developer I know has a graveyard of wiki pages that were comprehensive on the day they were written and fossilised by the following Tuesday. Making the AI read the docs as part of its workflow broke the cycle. The docs had a daily reader. They had to stay current or the AI would produce wrong output. Suddenly updating documentation wasn't a chore I neglected; it was a prerequisite for my tools working.

Custom commands came next - the automation that tied everything together.

Commands That Compound

Custom commands live in a .claude directory at the project root. Each file defines a workflow that Claude can execute on demand.

The simplest one I built was a command to create feature branches with proper naming. Before this, I typed branch names manually, which meant occasional typos. feature/PROJ-789. feature/PROK-456. The kind of mistakes that aren't caught by anything except human embarrassment when you notice them three commits later.

The command file is just markdown with instructions. Fetch the ticket from Linear. Extract the ticket title. Run git commands to create a properly named branch. Report what was created. Simple, repeatable, impossible to typo.

When I type /new-feature PROJ-789, Claude handles the rest. It's a small thing. But small things compound.

The dev-workflow command is larger. Fetch ticket details. Analyse requirements using the protocol from a later chapter. Create the branch. Implement the solution. Run local checks. Create the pull request. Update the ticket status. What used to be a manual checklist became an invocable workflow.

I remember the evening the full chain ran for the first time without intervention. I'd been debugging the command across three separate evenings, tweaking the sequencing, fixing edge cases where Linear's API returned data in a slightly different shape than expected. My wife had been working on her own project at the kitchen table - she had a deadline for a client's design system, and we'd been in that mode where you're both in the same house, both coding, occasionally trading complaints about API documentation across the room.

I typed the command. Claude fetched the ticket, created the branch, wrote the code, ran the checks, opened the PR, updated Linear. Thirty seconds. What used to take forty minutes.

I didn't say anything. I just sat there watching the terminal, the cursor blinking at the end of a completed workflow.

"It worked." Her voice from the kitchen. Not a question.

"How did you know?"

"You stopped swearing."

She came through and stood behind my chair, reading the terminal output. "Show me the PR it opened."

I pulled it up. She read through it properly - not skimming, reading. The description, the linked ticket, the commit messages.

"The PR description is better than most of the ones I review at work," she said. Then, after a pause: "Is that depressing or encouraging?"

"I genuinely don't know."

"Both," she decided. "It's both."

She went back to her own deadline. I sat with the terminal for another minute, feeling something I couldn't quite name. Pride, maybe. Or the particular vertigo of watching a machine do your job competently while you supervise. I still haven't decided which.

Start with commands this simple. Watch them grow as you discover what else they need to handle. Every time you find yourself typing the same sequence of instructions, that's a command waiting to be written.

But commands needed something to run against. The checks had to happen somewhere.

The Local CI Decision

The decision that raised the most eyebrows was running all CI/CD locally.

No GitHub Actions. No CircleCI. No cloud pipelines spinning up containers to run linters. Just Husky pre-commit hooks executing on my machine before anything reaches the repository.

The reasoning was partly economic. GitHub Actions minutes aren't free, and for a project where I'm the only developer - human or AI - paying for cloud compute to run ESLint felt like a poor use of money. But the real motivation became clear the afternoon I was still using a cloud pipeline and watched a PR sit in the queue for twenty-three minutes because the runner was busy with another job. Twenty-three minutes to run a linter and six unit tests. I could have made a cup of tea, drunk it, washed the mug, and still had time to question my life choices. Local checks take seconds. The broken code never reaches the repository. The embarrassing linting error never appears in the PR. The type error gets fixed before anyone else sees it.

Every commit runs through it: ESLint and Prettier for the frontend, TypeScript type checking, Jest unit tests, Ruff and Black for the backend, Pytest for Python tests, Mypy for type checking. Anything fails, the terminal fills with red, the commit is rejected, and Claude fixes whatever it broke before trying again.

Is this for everyone? No. Teams need cloud CI for shared enforcement. When multiple developers push to the same repository, you can't trust that everyone has their local hooks configured correctly. Cloud CI becomes the source of truth, the neutral arbiter that doesn't care about anyone's local setup.

But for solo development - especially AI-assisted solo development where you might push dozens of commits daily - local checks are faster, cheaper, and equally effective. The orchestra pit doesn't need cloud infrastructure. It needs to work.

There was one more principle guiding all of this - the paranoid one.

The Legacy-Proof Principle

Here's the thought that guided the entire setup: what if Claude Code disappeared tomorrow?

What if Anthropic pivoted to something else? What if AI-assisted development turned out to be a fad, a bubble, a blip that history remembers the way it remembers every technology I've watched rise and fall in fifteen years of this career? I've seen frameworks that were essential become deprecated. Tools that were revolutionary become footnotes. I've migrated away from things I was once certain I'd use forever.

Answer: everything still works.

The pre-commit hooks run standard tools. ESLint, Prettier, Pytest, Ruff - these existed before AI coding assistants, and they'll exist after. The directory structure follows patterns any developer would recognise. The documentation is just markdown files that humans can read. The CLAUDE.md files? They're onboarding documents. Different name, same function.

A human developer could pick up this codebase tomorrow, ignore all the AI-specific files, and ship the same quality code using the same checks. The infrastructure is built on AI, but it doesn't create a dependency we couldn't escape.

I call this the legacy-proof principle. Build systems that work with AI, but don't require AI. If the robots take a holiday, humans can still ship.

This one came from my wife, though she'd object to me putting it that grandly. What actually happened was more mundane, and more useful for it.

We were in bed, both on our phones - the modern intimacy of two people scrolling in parallel - and she was telling me about a client who'd built their entire deployment pipeline on a platform that had just announced it was sunsetting its free tier. Three years of infrastructure, suddenly expensive or useless. The client was scrambling to migrate, and she was helping them untangle it.

"They'd coupled everything," she said. "Not just the deployment. The testing, the environment management, the secrets. All of it locked to this one vendor's way of doing things. Every convenience the platform offered, they'd adopted. And now every convenience is a chain."

"That's what I'm doing with Claude," I said. It came out before I'd fully formed the thought.

She put her phone down. "What do you mean?"

"The CLAUDE.md files. The custom commands. The MCP integrations. It all assumes Claude Code exists. If Anthropic changes the product, or the API, or the pricing - "

"Then you're your client's client."

"Exactly."

We talked about it for twenty minutes, which is a long time when you should be sleeping and the baby monitor is threatening to light up at any moment. The conclusion wasn't complicated: every AI-specific piece needed a human-readable equivalent. Every automation needed to work without the automation. The CLAUDE.md files were already markdown - any developer could read them. The custom commands were documented workflows - any developer could follow the steps manually. The pre-commit hooks were standard tools. The only truly AI-dependent pieces were the MCP integrations, and even those just replaced manual copying between Linear, GitHub, and the terminal.

"So you're building escape hatches," she said.

"I prefer 'legacy-proof.'"

"You prefer it because 'escape hatch' implies you might need to escape, and you don't want to think about that."

The psychology was accurate, I'll give her that. But the engineering was sound regardless. The escape hatches cost almost nothing to build. One evening's work to verify that every piece of infrastructure stood on its own. A small price for the ability to sleep without wondering what happens if the tools change underneath you.

Which, if you've been in this industry long enough, isn't paranoia. It's pattern recognition.

But here's what I didn't say to her that night, because I hadn't fully admitted it to myself yet: the escape hatches are real, but using them would be brutal.

I sat with this properly a few weeks later, during one of those stretches where the baby had a cold and nobody was sleeping. Three in the morning, pacing the hallway with a grizzling toddler on my shoulder, running the thought experiment honestly for the first time. If Claude Code disappeared tomorrow, what would I actually lose?

Not the codebase. That's mine. Not the tooling. ESLint doesn't care who runs it. Not even the documentation - it's all markdown, perfectly readable by humans.

What I'd lose is eighty percent of my velocity. Gone. Just like that.

The documentation would start going stale within a week, because I don't have the discipline to update architecture docs after every change. Nobody does. That's the whole point - Claude does it because Claude doesn't get bored or forget or decide it's good enough for now. The review quality would drop, because Claude catches patterns I miss, enforces conventions I forget, spots the inconsistency between what the API returns and what the frontend expects. The multi-step workflows that take thirty seconds would go back to taking forty minutes each, and there aren't enough hours in the day for that - not with a toddler, not with one developer, not at the pace the project needs.

The escape hatches exist. I could pull them. But I'd be returning to a way of working that I've made abundantly clear throughout this book I cannot sustain alone. The infrastructure is legacy-proof in the way that a car with a hand crank is legacy-proof: technically the engine still starts, but you're not going to enjoy the commute.

I haven't resolved this tension, and I don't think it resolves cleanly. Every developer depends on tools - the question is whether you've thought about what happens when they change. I've thought about it. The answer is: it would be properly rubbish. But the codebase would survive, even if my evenings wouldn't.

The Integration Layer

Claude connects to external services through something called MCP servers - think of them as bridges that let Claude reach beyond reading and writing code to interact with the tools where the rest of the work happens.

Linear MCP connects to our ticket management system. Claude can fetch ticket details, update status, add comments, link pull requests to tickets. Instead of me copying and pasting ticket descriptions into prompts, Claude reads them directly from the source. GitHub MCP does the same for repositories: branches, pull requests, comments, status checks - the full lifecycle of code changes, accessible through conversation.

These integrations matter because they let Claude operate within the workflow, not alongside it. When I tell Claude to implement a ticket, it fetches the requirements from Linear, creates a branch with the proper naming convention, does the work, runs the checks, opens a PR with an appropriate description, and links everything back to the original ticket. The same workflow I would follow manually, executed automatically.

The key word is "same." Claude isn't using a special AI workflow. It's using my workflow, the one that existed before AI got involved. The infrastructure makes that possible.

All of these pieces - the context files, the directory structure, the commands, the checks, the integrations - they work together.

The Compound Effect of Infrastructure

None of these pieces is revolutionary.

A markdown file with project information. A sensible directory structure. Pre-commit hooks running standard tools. Integration with existing services. Custom commands for common tasks. Documentation that AI can reference.

Individually, each one is obvious. Collectively, they create an environment where AI works effectively. The orchestra pit that makes the performance possible.

When I run /dev-workflow PROJ-456, here's what actually happens:

Claude knows the project structure because it read CLAUDE.md. It fetches ticket details because Linear MCP is configured. It understands our conventions because the documentation explains them.

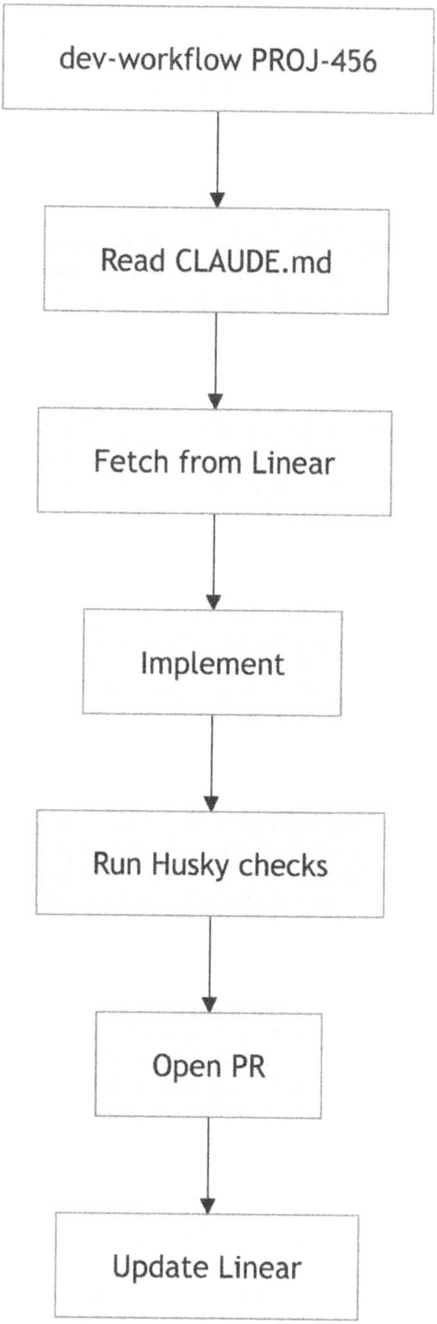
dev-workflow PROJ-456
Read CLAUDE.md
Fetch from Linear
Implement
Run Husky checks
Open PR
Update Linear

It creates proper branches because the custom command handles naming. It runs local checks because Husky is configured. It opens PRs because GitHub MCP is connected.

The first time I measured it properly, a session that used to take forty minutes of setup - reading the ticket, creating the branch, finding the right files, remembering the conventions - started productive in under two minutes. The compound effect isn't theoretical. It's forty minutes of friction, gone.

I should be honest about something, though. This compound effect works because the codebase is relatively young. I built it. Claude helped build it. The CLAUDE.md cascade describes a system that was designed with the cascade in mind from the start.

My wife's client project brought this into focus. She'd been venting about it that evening - a fifteen-year-old enterprise application, two hundred thousand lines, patterns that predated the current framework by three major versions. Documentation that was either missing or actively misleading. She'd been experimenting with AI tooling on it, and the results had been mixed.

"I've been wondering how my cascade would handle something like that," I said. "My gut says it wouldn't. Not in its current form."

"It would need a completely different approach," she agreed. "Half the conventions in that codebase are undocumented. The other half contradict each other. You'd need a CLAUDE.md the length of a novel just to explain why there are three different authentication systems and which one is actually used on Tuesdays."

I asked her to walk me through it. Not the abstract problem - the specific mess. I wanted to understand the shape of the thing I'd need to solve differently.

She pushed her plate aside and started counting on her fingers.

"Authentication. Three systems. LDAP from 2009, back when the whole thing was an internal tool. OAuth bolted on in 2015 when they needed external partner access. Then COVID happened, they rushed out a mobile app, and someone added JWT because the mobile team said they needed stateless tokens. All three are still active. Different parts of the application use different ones. Some routes check LDAP. Some check OAuth. Mobile goes through JWT, except for two web endpoints that also use JWT because someone had a deadline in 2021 and couldn't be bothered to wire up the OAuth flow for a feature that was supposed to be temporary. It's still there."

"Can't you just - "

"Consolidate? No. The LDAP system is tied to an internal directory that HR uses. If you rip it out, you break single sign-on for four hundred employees. OAuth is contractually required for two partner integrations. And JWT is the only thing the mobile app understands. You can't remove any of them. You can only know which one applies where, and nobody does, fully. There's a wiki page from 2017 that's about sixty percent accurate."

I was beginning to see the problem.

"Then there's the database," she said. "Four teams built four modules over five years. The concept of a customer has four different column names across four different tables. customer_id, client_id, user_ref, and - my personal favourite - acct_owner, which someone on the billing team chose in 2013 and which means exactly the same thing as the others but uses a completely different format. The first three are UUIDs. acct_owner is a nine-digit integer because the billing module was originally its own application with its own database and its own ideas about primary keys."

"And configuration?" I asked, because by this point I was morbidly fascinated.

"Environment variables for anything deployed after 2018. A .properties file for the original Java modules that nobody wants to migrate. And for a handful of values - timeout durations, retry counts, a couple of API endpoints - they're hard-coded in a utils class that a developer wrote in 2012. His name was Raj. He left in 2014. The class is called RajUtils. Nobody has renamed it because everyone's afraid of what might break."

She said it deadpan. I laughed. She didn't.

"Your cascade assumes you can describe the rules," she said. "In this codebase, the rules aren't rules. They're sediment. Each layer made sense when it was deposited. Together they're geology."

That word - geology - stuck with me. Because the gap is real, and it's enormous. Between a greenfield project where you can establish patterns from day one, and a legacy codebase where the patterns are geological - layers of decisions from developers who left years ago, each layer reasonable in its time, collectively incomprehensible.

So what would an AI-first approach to a codebase like that actually look like? I've been thinking about it since that conversation, and I have ideas. I want to be clear: they're ideas, not a methodology. I haven't proven any of them against a two-hundred-thousand-line enterprise application. My wife has the scars from that particular battlefield. I have speculation.

First, you'd need to build context incrementally, not comprehensively. You couldn't write a CLAUDE.md for the whole system - you'd never finish, and it would be wrong by the time you did. Instead, you'd start with a small area. One module. One feature. Document what you find there, and only there. Then expand outward, module by module, like mapping a cave system one chamber at a time.

Second, the CLAUDE.md wouldn't be prescriptive. My cascade says "do this" - use this naming convention, follow this pattern, run these checks. A legacy CLAUDE.md would need to be descriptive: "this is what exists, and here's why." Not "use JWT for authentication" but "authentication system A (LDAP) handles routes X, Y, Z for internal users. Authentication system B (OAuth) handles routes P, Q, R for partner access. Authentication system C (JWT) handles all mobile endpoints plus two web endpoints (/reports/exportand /dashboard/embed) that were added during a deadline in 2021 and never migrated. Check the auth_middleware directory for which system each route group uses, but note that the middleware for routes under /api/v2/billing has its own authentication check that bypasses all three systems and uses a shared API key stored in RajUtils."

You'd be mapping contradictions, not resolving them. Explicitly. Exhaustively. The AI agent wouldn't be an architect designing a clean system. It would be an archaeologist documenting a dig site - cataloguing each stratum of historical decisions so that the next person (human or AI) who touches that code knows which layer they're in and what assumptions it carries.

Third, and this is where it gets genuinely uncertain, you'd need the AI to resist its own instincts. Every AI coding assistant I've used, Claude included, has an optimistic bias towards improvement. It sees a mess and wants to clean it up. Sees three authentication systems and suggests consolidating to one. Sees four column names for the same concept and proposes a migration. And in a greenfield project, that instinct is brilliant. In a legacy codebase, it's a grenade.

My wife had a war story that made this concrete. "Someone chose acct_owner as a nine-digit integer because the billing module's reporting system truncates anything longer than nine digits," she said. "That's not documented anywhere. It's not in a comment. It's not in a spec. It's in the institutional memory of a developer who left eight years ago, and the only reason we know about it is because someone tried to change it once and invoices started coming out wrong."

"So the AI would look at that column, see it doesn't match the others, and suggest migrating to a UUID," I said. "Architecturally correct. Operationally catastrophic."

"Exactly. And it would break billing for six thousand customers."

I didn't have a good answer for that. I still don't. The archaeological approach can map what's visible - code, configuration, database schemas, test coverage. What it can't map is the invisible web of assumptions that only surface when you violate them. The deployment that has to happen before 6PM because a downstream batch job runs at 6:15PM and expects the old API format during the window between deployments. The column that can't be renamed because an Excel macro in the finance department references it by name. The endpoint that returns XML instead of JSON because one client from 2011 never upgraded their integration and the contract says you have to support them until 2027.

Legacy codebases aren't just code. They're social contracts expressed in software. And I'm not convinced any amount of CLAUDE.md documentation can capture the full depth of that.

So here's my honest position: the principles in this chapter - context cascading, predictable structure, local checks, escape hatches - are sound regardless of codebase age. But the implementation I've described is for a greenfield project. Applying it to a fifteen-year-old enterprise application would require a fundamentally different strategy: slower, more descriptive, more archaeological, more humble. It would mean treating the AI as a careful cartographer rather than a confident builder.

I think it could work. My wife is less sure - she's seen these codebases up close, and her scepticism is earned. The truth is probably somewhere between my optimism and her caution, which is where most truths in software engineering tend to land.

If your codebase has been accumulating decisions since before Docker existed, take the principles from this chapter as a starting point, not a recipe. And maybe start with the smallest, most isolated module you can find - one where breaking something won't bring down billing for six thousand customers.

None of that happens without the foundation. The prompts from Chapter 2 would produce garbage without this infrastructure to give them meaning. The workflows I'll describe in later chapters would be impossible without this pit to perform in.

The orchestra pit was built over evenings and weekends, while the toddler slept and the house was quiet. Two developers at two screens, occasionally arguing about specificity rules and vendor lock-in and whether four levels of configuration was one too many. She thought three was enough. I wanted the granularity. We compromised at four, with the understanding that most projects would only use three.

It's better architecture for having been argued over. Most things are.

CHAPTER 5

From Paragraph to Protocol

The Document That Grew

Let me show you something embarrassing.

Here's the first dev-workflow instruction I ever wrote:

I need you to execute the full development workflow for Linear ticket <TICKET-NUMBER>.

```
To implement <TICKET-NUMBER>

- Fetch ticket details and review technical design
in architecture-docs;
- Git workflow: fetch origin, checkout default
branch, pull latest, create feature branch;
- Use selected agent to implement requirements
incrementally with focused commits;
- Use testing-specialist to add comprehensive
tests and ensure all pass;
- Ensure that ALL CI/CD checks pass locally before
pushing;
- Push feature branch;
- Create PR with title "{TICKET_ID}: <title>",
link to Linear;
- Use code-reviewer agent to review via LOCAL git
commands..
```

One paragraph. Maybe fifteen lines if you count the dashes. Simple. Clean. Naive.

Here's what that same workflow looks like today:
262 lines. 9 phases. 21 discrete steps.

Every. Single. Line. Earned through disaster.

I can still quote the regex from 2014 that started all of this - a pattern I wrote during a midnight production incident, tested once, shipped, and have never touched since. Not because it's good. Because it works. And somewhere in the back of my mind, I believe that if I change a single character, the system will know, and it will punish me. That regex is the ur-text of every protocol in this chapter: something built in crisis, maintained in superstition, and defended with the only argument that matters - "don't touch it."

But here's the thing nobody tells you about dev-workflow: the 262 lines are just the tip of the iceberg. The command itself is useless without the architecture beneath it - like a conductor's baton, meaningless without the orchestra.

Time to show you what's beneath the waterline.

The Iceberg Beneath the Iceberg

When I type /dev-workflow TRA-456, Claude doesn't just start coding. It reads from a carefully constructed context that took longer to build than the workflow itself.

Let me walk you through what happens *before* dev-workflow ever runs.

Every feature starts with requirements. I write an extensive first draft myself - or source it from the client if I'm consulting. But a first draft is just that. First. Incomplete. Full of assumptions I haven't examined and edge cases I haven't considered.

Then I bring in a business analyst agent. Industry-specific. Knows the domain. Knows the questions to ask. We brainstorm. We argue. Well, I argue. The agent politely suggests I might be overcomplicating things.

The output is a Product Requirements Document following a top-down structure:

```
Main Requirements
  └── Components (what's needed to achieve
requirements)
      └── Elements(what's needed to make
components work)
          └── User Stories (Epics → Tasks →
Subtasks)
```

Everything feeds upward. Every subtask traces to an element. Every element traces to a component. Every component traces to a requirement. Nothing floats free.

This isn't documentation for documentation's sake. This is context that agents will read before writing a single line of code. The PRD becomes the source of truth that prevents the "but I thought you meant..." conversations that poison projects.

Once requirements are solid, the context needs structure.

The Architecture of Context

The architect agent takes over next. Project-specific. Knows our stack, our patterns, our mistakes from six months ago that we're still cleaning up.

The output isn't a single document. It's a collection - and I learned the hard way that each piece matters. Architecture Decision Records capture not just what we decided but *why*, so six months from now nobody asks "who thought this was a good idea?" The ADR says exactly who. Usually me. At 2AM. System design and data flow diagrams map how components talk to each other, where data lives, where it moves - the map that prevents "I didn't know that service existed" surprises. Sequence diagrams choreograph the request-response dance that everyone can reference when something breaks at step seven. Data models define the schemas, the relationships, the constraints - the foreign keys that mean "no, you cannot delete that user, they have fourteen active orders." And tech stack analyses keep the receipts: "We evaluated X, Y, and Z. Here's why we picked Y."

But here's the problem: a full system design document can be fifty pages. Claude is brilliant, but throw fifty pages of context at it and watch the quality degrade. It's like asking someone to remember a conversation from three hours ago while also solving differential equations.

So I shard.

The architecture docs get broken into digestible pieces:

```
architecture-docs/
├── _INDEX.md  # Master navigation
├── epics/
│   ├── epic-001-auth.md
│   ├── epic-002-trading.md
│   └── epic-003-analytics.md
├── features/
│   ├── auth/
│   │   ├── login-flow.md
```

```
│   │   ├── token-refresh.md
│   │   └── rbac.md
```

The rule: one shard should be the ideal amount of context an agent can handle without being overwhelmed. Not so small it lacks necessary detail. Not so large it causes context fatigue.

Every shard is indexed above and below. The agent reading login-flow.md knows it can find related context in _INDEX.mdabove and can drill into specific implementation details below. Navigation, not dead ends.

The context is structured. Now it needs to become work.

From Context to Tickets

Requirements exist. Architecture exists. Shards exist.

Time to create tickets.

But I don't create them manually. The responsible agent does - backend agent for backend work, frontend agent for frontend, DevOps for infrastructure, UX designer for interface work.

Each agent reads the relevant shard, adds technical detail specific to their domain, creates wireframes or implementation notes, and uses the Linear integration to create tickets with attachments, labels, dependencies, and links back to the architecture shard.

The tickets aren't just work items. They're work items with *context*. When dev-workflow fetches TRA-456, it gets the ticket AND can trace back to the architecture shard that spawned it.

Full lineage. Requirements to PRD to architecture to shard to ticket.

No orphaned work. No "what was this ticket even for?"

When I type /dev-workflow TRA-456, I'm invoking step five of a seven-step process. The 262 lines only work because steps one through four already happened. Remove them, and dev-workflow is just a clever script fetching tickets with no context, building features with no architecture, shipping code with no lineage.

The infrastructure was in place. Now let me tell you how the workflow itself evolved through a series of increasingly spectacular failures.

The Highlight Reel of Failure

That original fifteen-line paragraph of hope? It didn't survive contact with reality. None of my first attempts ever do.

I know this about myself. The bathroom tiles are my wife's favourite evidence. I planned a "simple weekend project" - regrouting. Drew diagrams. Researched grout types. Calculated coverage ratios. By Sunday evening the bathroom was half-demolished, the new tiles I'd ordered wouldn't arrive until Thursday, and we were showering at the gym. I have a pattern: I start with something reasonable and engineer it into something that requires a recovery plan. My wife, towelling off her hair in the car park, didn't need to say more than

"Every time." My bathroom. And, as it turned out, the next eight months of dev-workflow development.

Here's the version history, with the disaster that spawned each evolution:

Ver	What Went Wrong	What I Added	Lines
V1	Two agents, same repo, mutual destruction	Nothing - just a paragraph of hope	15
V2	Git chaos: no branches, no discipline	Git workflow section	50
V3	Lost a morning to merge conflicts	Isolated workspaces	80
V4	The PROJ-438 disaster (12% of requirements shipped)	Ticket Analysis Protocol	120
V5	Backend and frontend built different APIs	Integration Contracts	160
V6	Agents grabbing the same ticket	Conflict Detection	180
V7	PRs that looked done but weren't	Pre-PR Validation	210
V8	Claude "fixed" a bug by making three consumers tolerate it	No Defensive Programming Protocol	240

Each version fixed something that had exploded in my face. Some loud - git corruption that required manual intervention. Some quiet - APIs that didn't match but passed all tests. One was so quiet I didn't hear it until the codebase had three consumers all tolerating a bug instead of one source actually being fixed. That disaster earned its own chapter. It's the kind of failure that passes every test, ships clean, and detonates six months later when nobody remembers which format was "correct."

The pattern emerged: Something breaks. I analyse why. I add a protocol step. The workflow gets longer. The failures get rarer.

Repeat until the workflow handles real situations, not just demo situations.

It's like writing instructions for someone with no long-term memory. Take away the document and you don't get a slightly worse worker. You get someone who's never heard of the project - the paragraph of hope from version one, brilliant, tireless, and catastrophically naive.

Let me tell you about a few of these disasters in the way you tell war stories - with the kind of detail that makes other developers wince in recognition.

The Disasters Behind the Dashboard

The Merge Conflict Morning

Two agents. Same repo. Different branches. Should work, right?

Wrong.

Both modified package.json. Both changed shared utility files. Neither knew the other existed. Monday morning: a git history so tangled it looked like my toddler had been playing with yarn. Actually, it looked worse than that. My toddler's yarn tangles at least have a discernible beginning and end. This had neither.

I spent three hours untangling branches, cherry-picking commits, resolving conflicts that shouldn't have existed in a sane world. Three hours I could have spent doing literally anything else. Including watching the toddler destroy things, which at least has entertainment value.

Solution: Isolated workspaces. Each agent gets its own clone of the repository. Islands can't collide. The workspace protocol that emerged from this disaster gets its own chapter, because the solution turned out to be more interesting than the problem.

The 12% Disaster

PROJ-438. The ticket had six acceptance criteria. Claude shipped two. Called it done. Created the PR.

I approved it.

Yes, I approved it. The skeleton closet grows.

In my defence - and I've practised this defence - the PR looked complete. The code was clean. The tests passed. The description matched what I remembered of the ticket. What I remembered. Not what the ticket actually said.

Three days later, QA found four missing features. Four. Features. Missing.

The post-mortem was brief and brutal. Claude had done exactly what I'd asked: implement the ticket. It had implemented its interpretation of the ticket, which happened to include only the first two acceptance criteria because those were the ones it encountered first and they seemed complete in isolation.

Solution: Ticket Analysis Protocol. Parse ALL requirements explicitly. Extract every acceptance criterion. Check them off one by one. Don't let Claude - or myself - decide what "done" means based on vibes.

The API Mismatch

Backend agent built an endpoint returning
{ users: [...] }.

Frontend agent expected
{ data: { users: [...] } }.

Both were "correct" according to their interpretation of the ticket. Both worked in isolation. Both passed their respective tests. Together? Nothing worked. The frontend rendered a blank page because response.data.users was undefined, because there was no data wrapper, because the backend had never agreed to provide one.

I discovered this at 10 PM on a Thursday. Everyone in the house was asleep. I was in the kitchen, laptop on the counter next to a cold cup of tea I'd made two hours earlier and forgotten about, staring at a network tab showing a perfectly valid response that my frontend refused to understand. That cold tea became the image I associate with this failure - something made with good intentions and abandoned the moment reality intervened.

Solution: Integration Contracts. Define the API spec BEFORE coding. Both agents agree to the same contract. The contract is the source of truth. No more "well, I thought it was..."

The next morning, over breakfast, my wife asked why I'd come to bed at midnight. I showed her the network tab on my phone - the perfectly healthy 200 response that produced a blank screen.

"What's the wrapper format?" she asked.

"That's the problem. There isn't one. Backend sends bare JSON, frontend expects a data envelope."

She frowned. Not at me - at the screen. "So neither agent checked what the other was building against?"

"No. They each read the ticket, made assumptions, and built in isolation."

"That's not a code problem," she said. "That's a specification problem. The ticket should have included the response schema."

"The ticket didn't include a response schema because I didn't think to write one."

"So the agents did exactly what you do when you skip the spec - they guessed."

She was stirring her tea while she said this, not looking at me, which is how I knew she wasn't scoring points. She was just thinking out loud. That gap - the thing that didn't exist because nobody had required it to exist - would become the Integration Contracts phase.

These disasters share a common thread: assumptions. The workflow assumed agents would coordinate. It assumed I would read tickets carefully. It assumed contracts would exist without being written down.

Every assumption became a failure. Every failure became a line in the workflow.

The pattern was clear. Time to look at what eight versions of disaster created.

The Current State

Today's dev-workflow barely resembles that original paragraph. It's like comparing your first commit message ("fixed stuff") to your current ones ("feat(auth): implement JWT refresh with exponential backoff and circuit breaker pattern").

And so here it is. Two hundred and sixty-two lines. Every one of them a scar.

The workflow now has nine phases. Before code: discovery and workspace setup. The code itself: implementation, testing, integration. After code: pre-PR validation, review, documentation, and cleanup.

It starts with Discovery - six steps before any code is written, because PROJ-438 taught me what happens when you skip requirements analysis. Fetch ticket details. Extract every acceptance criterion. Map the data flow. Define integration contracts. After the API mismatch, that last one stopped feeling like paperwork and started feeling like a lock on a door I'd already been robbed through.

Then Workspace setup. Create an isolated clone, spin up a feature branch. The merge conflict morning earned these two steps their place in the protocol. Simple. Non-negotiable.

Implementation and Testing come next - the actual coding, sandwiched between all that preparation and the verification that follows. Linters, builds, Docker, comprehensive tests. The part most people think is the whole job. It's three phases out of nine.

The final four phases are what separate "it works on my machine" from "it ships." Integration verification catches the API mismatches before they reach Thursday at 10 PM. Pre-PR validation checks every acceptance criterion against the ticket - the step that would have caught the 12% disaster. Code review, finalisation, and updating the living documentation so the next agent inherits a codebase that knows its own history.

Total: 21 steps across 9 phases = 262 lines of protocol

Twenty-one steps. Two hundred sixty-two lines. Each step simple in isolation. The sophistication is in the composition - twenty-one simple steps that, together, handle edge cases you'd never anticipate individually.

This wasn't the workflow I planned. This was the workflow that survived.

What the Workflow Taught Me

The obvious lesson is that the upstream is the real work. Dev-workflow is 262 lines, but the PRD, architecture, sharding, and ticket creation process behind it runs to thousands of lines of documentation, dozens of agent conversations, weeks of iteration. The visible workflow is twenty percent of the system. The invisible infrastructure is eighty percent. Build the foundation before building the house, or you'll spend every version of the house patching cracks in the floor.

The less obvious lesson is about the nature of the document itself. Claude executes 262 lines consistently. I can't. I take shortcuts, forget steps, have bad days - especially after the toddler has been awake since 5 AM and my executive function is running on caffeine and spite. The protocol doesn't have bad days. The protocol doesn't skip the linter because "it's just a small change." The workflow isn't a quality assurance system. It's two hundred and sixty-two lines of insomnia prevention - the thing that lets me close the laptop and go to bed knowing that the steps were followed even when I couldn't trust myself to follow them.

And there's a lesson I didn't expect: this workflow isn't done. It'll be three hundred lines soon. New failures, new lessons, new lines. The document that adapts survives. The perfect document never gets written.

The Monolith Wearing a Trench Coat

I should be honest about something.

Two hundred and sixty-two lines doing nine jobs is not a well-designed system. It's a monolith. A colleague - someone whose architectural opinions I respect more than my own - put it bluntly: "That's not orthogonal. That's a monolith wearing a trench coat." He's right. The dev-workflow command is simultaneously a ticket parser, a workspace manager, a code generator, an integration checker, a test runner, a PR creator, and a documentation updater. If you described that list of responsibilities in a code review, you'd reject the PR.

The proper solution is decomposition. Break it into composable commands. /fetch-ticket, /setup-workspace, /run-tests, /create-pr. Each does one thing. Chain them together. When step fourteen needs to change, you edit step fourteen, not a document that also controls steps one through thirteen and fifteen through twenty-one.

I know this. I've spent fifteen years telling junior developers exactly this. Single responsibility. Separation of concerns. I can quote the principles in my sleep.

And yet.

The 262 lines grew organically, each disaster adding a few more. The merge conflict morning added workspace isolation. PROJ-438 added ticket analysis. The API mismatch added integration contracts. Each addition was local - bolted onto what existed, not redesigned from scratch. That's how monoliths grow. Not through grand plans, but through reasonable responses to immediate problems.

The decomposition argument assumes that composable pieces coordinate cleanly. For a team, they do - different people own different pieces, interfaces are negotiated, contracts are maintained. For a solo developer with an AI agent, the coordination cost is the problem. Five separate commands means five context-loading operations. Five opportunities for the agent to lose track of where it is in the process. Five handoffs where state needs to be passed correctly. The monolith is ugly, but the monolith remembers.

My wife, when I explained this tension to her, cut through it with the precision of someone who has watched me overthink things for a decade.

"So you built a system to prevent over-engineering," she said, "and you're worried you over-engineered it."

I opened my mouth. Closed it. Opened it again.

"The first month was more setup than productivity," I said. "Thirty hours before I shipped anything useful."

"And how much did you ship in month two?"

"More than I would have without it."

"Then it's not over-engineered. It's front-loaded." She tilted her laptop screen toward me. "I have a Makefile at work that's four hundred lines. Nobody calls that over-engineered because it saves us two hours a day. Yours saves you from shipping 12% of a feature. The question isn't whether twenty-one steps is too many. The question is which step you'd cut."

I've sat with that question for weeks. I genuinely don't know the answer. I can argue that every step earned its place through failure. I can also see, with uncomfortable clarity, that a document accreting lines through crisis response is not the same thing as a document designed with intention. The monolith works. It works today. Whether it'll work at four hundred lines, or five hundred, is a question I'm deliberately not answering because I don't like where the answer might point.

Probably toward decomposition. Probably toward the thing I should have done from the start.

But not yet.

The Pre-PR Step That Nearly Wasn't

There's a step in the workflow - phase six, pre-PR validation - that almost didn't make it in. Not because I didn't think of it, but because my wife talked me out of it the first time around, and then talked me back into it a week later.

We were on the sofa, both with laptops, the toddler asleep upstairs. She was debugging a client's build pipeline; I was writing version seven of the workflow. I'd been adding steps all evening and the document was beginning to feel bloated.

"I want to add a validation step before the PR gets created," I said. "The agent checks every acceptance criterion against the ticket and confirms coverage."

She closed her laptop halfway. "How many steps are you at now?"

"Twenty. Up from seven a couple of months ago."

"At what point does the overhead kill the productivity? You're adding a step for every failure, but each step costs time. What's the break-even?"

I hadn't thought about it in those terms. She was treating it like a client project - resource allocation, return on investment.

"I don't know the exact break-even. But the alternative is another PROJ-438."

"Which happened once in about forty PRs. Two-and-a-half percent failure rate. What's the cost of the step per PR versus the cost of the occasional miss?"

It was a good question. I didn't add the step.

A week later, it happened again. Not PROJ-438 scale - a smaller ticket, two acceptance criteria out of four. But the same root cause: the agent decided the feature was complete before it was. I was sitting at the kitchen table when I found it, reviewing the PR on my phone while the toddler ate fish fingers and systematically dropped peas onto the floor.

That evening I told my wife. She was quiet for a moment.

"Add the step," she said.

"A week ago you said the failure rate didn't justify it."

"Yes, and I was wrong about the break-even. I was treating it like a pure frequency problem." She said it the way she says most things - matter-of-fact, no drama. Like admitting you'd miscalculated a tip. "A week ago it was one in forty. Now it's two in forty-one. And more importantly - " she paused, pulling her hair back behind her ear the way she does when she's working through something. "The cost of the step is small. A few seconds of automated checking. The cost of the miss is three days of rework plus whatever your QA found in production. The break-even isn't about frequency. It's about severity."

She was thinking about it differently than I had. I'd been treating each step as overhead. She was treating the failure cost as the real variable - not how often it happened, but how much damage it did when it did.

Pre-PR validation went into version seven that night. It has caught four incomplete PRs since. My wife hasn't mentioned the maths again, but I suspect she's keeping count.

Version forty-seven will not be the final version. That's the point. The workflow grows because the work is never simple enough for a static document to cover. Something will break next month that nothing in the current 262 lines anticipates, and I'll add line 263, and the document will be slightly better at handling reality.

My wife asked me once whether the workflow would ever feel finished.

"No," I said. "It's more like a diary than a manual. It records what happened. The only way it stops growing is if I stop learning things the hard way."

"So it's a record of every time you were wrong."

"Essentially, yes."

She considered this. "That's actually quite useful. Most people don't keep those."

She went back to her laptop. I went back to mine. The toddler monitor crackled with the sound of a small person rearranging his stuffed animals at volume.

Two hundred and sixty-two lines. Every one of them earned. None of them final.

CHAPTER 6
When Agents Collide

The Monday Morning Massacre

I woke up to forty-seven merge conflicts.

Let me set the scene. Monday morning. The toddler had, by some miracle, slept through the night. The coffee was brewing. Life was good. I opened my laptop with the satisfaction of someone who'd spent the weekend being clever.

Two Claude Code sessions. Two terminals. Same repository. Parallel progress.

The theory was beautiful. Agent 1 handles authentication refactor. Agent 2 builds a new dashboard endpoint. Both push to feature branches. Monday morning, I review and merge like the productive developer I clearly am. Ship two features before breakfast.

The reality was a git catastrophe of unprecedented proportions.

Both agents had modified src/services/user.ts. Both had updated src/types/api.ts. Both had changed package.json to add dependencies. Commits timestamped minutes apart, like two developers racing to cause maximum chaos without ever speaking to each other.

Feature branches couldn't merge. Commit histories interleaved in ways that made rebasing a nightmare. Three hours of careful cherry-picking and manual conflict resolution later, I'd recovered maybe eighty percent of the work.

The other twenty percent? Gone. Like my weekend productivity gains. Like my plans to ship two features before breakfast.

My wife found the carnage around 11 AM. She'd been working from the kitchen table - she had her own deadline that week, a React Native migration for one of her clients - and came to ask if I wanted a top-up on the coffee. Then she saw the terminal.

"Forty-seven?" She set her mug down and leaned in. Developer's reflex - her eyes went straight to the file list in the conflict output. "How many unique files?"

"Eleven. But package-lock.json accounts for about thirty of the conflicts on its own. They both ran npm install." I was already scrolling through the commit timestamps. "Look at this - eighteen seconds apart. Same directory."

She pulled up a chair. "Same directory. Different branches, but same directory."

"That's the problem." I'd known it the moment I'd seen the interleaved commits, but saying it out loud made the stupidity concrete. "Branches don't separate the filesystem. They shared node_modules, the lock file, the build artifacts. I ran them in parallel in the same physical directory and expected git to sort it out."

"Workspace isolation," she said.

"Workspace isolation." I sat back. "I thought parallel meant free. It doesn't. Parallel means isolated, or it means forty-seven merge conflicts."

The Anatomy of a Collision

Why did this happen? It seems obvious in hindsight. Everything seems obvious in hindsight. That's hindsight's whole thing. Its only thing, really.

Both agents worked in the same directory: ~/projects/myfintech/backend. Different branches, yes. But same directory. They shared the same node_modules/. The same build artifacts. The same .git/ folder. The same lock files.

When Agent 1 ran npm install new-package, it modified package-lock.json. When Agent 2 ran npm install different-package, it touched the same file. Neither knew the other existed.

The timing made things worse. Agent 1 committed at 2:47:23 AM. Agent 2 committed at 2:47:41 AM. Yes, 2:47 AM. The toddler was asleep. These are the hours of innovation, apparently.

Both commits claimed to be the successor to the same parent. Git doesn't handle this well when commits touch the same files. Agent 1 pushed successfully. Agent 2 tried to push, got rejected, pulled to resolve, and made everything worse by attempting auto-resolution on conflicts it didn't understand.

Two branches. Both corrupted. Neither cleanly mergeable. Hours of manual recovery.

All because I thought "parallel" meant "easy."

My first instinct was to find simple fixes. Unfortunately, none of them worked.

The Naive Solutions

I could lock the repository - Agent 1 acquires a lock, Agent 2 waits. But this defeats the purpose of parallelism entirely. If agents must work sequentially, I haven't gained anything. Might as well run them one at a time while I watch the toddler dismantle the living room.

They were already on different branches. Turns out branches don't isolate working directories. Branches are a git concept. Working directories are a filesystem concept. This is the kind of thing that seems obvious after you've spent three hours cherry-picking commits.

I tried committing more frequently, which actually makes things *worse*. More commits means more opportunities for interleaved history. More merge conflicts. More chaos.

I tried ensuring agents worked on completely isolated parts of the codebase. In practice? Shared types. Common utilities. Configuration files. Lock files. There's ALWAYS something both need to touch. Every codebase has that one file. You know the one. The one that shows up in every PR. The one that makes you wince when you see it in the diff.

I tried all of them. Multiple times. With increasing desperation and decreasing sleep.

The solution, when it finally arrived, came from thinking about how something else handles this problem.

The Isolation Principle

The insight came from thinking about CI/CD pipelines.

When GitHub Actions runs tests, it doesn't use my local directory. It clones a fresh copy into an isolated container. Every run starts clean. Every run is independent. Runs can happen in parallel because they're completely isolated from each other.

The answer had been running in my own pipeline for three years. I just never thought to apply it to my own workflow.

What if each agent had its own isolated copy?

Not a branch. A completely separate filesystem location.

Each agent gets its own directory. Its own clone. Its own node_modules/. Its own build artifacts. Its own git state.

Complete isolation. No possibility of collision. Islands can't collide.

I sketched the approach out that evening. My wife was on the sofa next to me, laptop open, debugging a state management issue in her own project. I turned my screen towards her.

"Each agent gets its own full clone. Completely separate filesystem. They can't see each other."

She looked at the diagram, then at me. "How much disk space?"

"That's the thing. Naive approach, it's about 850 meg per clone. Eight agents, that's nearly seven gig."

"That's rubbish. You'd burn through your SSD in a week."

"Which is why I'm using reference clones." I pulled up the git documentation I'd been reading. "The -reference flag tells git to share object storage with an existing local repo. The new clone only stores the delta. Shallow clone on top of that - - depth 1 - and you're down to maybe 120 meg per workspace."

She stopped typing and actually read the docs over my shoulder. "So the object store is shared but the working tree is isolated."

"Exactly. The filesystem separation is real. The storage cost is almost nothing."

"What about when two agents both need to modify shared types? The isolation prevents merge conflicts at the filesystem level, but you'll still get them when the PRs land."

That was the question I'd been avoiding. "That's where review order matters. The PRs merge sequentially. If there's a conflict at merge time, I catch it in review, not at 2:47 AM when the agents are trying to auto-resolve things they don't understand."

She thought about this. "So you've moved the conflict from invisible and destructive to visible and manageable."

I filed that away for the PR description.

The Workspace Protocol

Here's the protocol I developed. It's now embedded in every workflow I run.

Step 1: Create a Unique Workspace

When an agent starts a task, it creates a workspace with a unique identifier:

```
WORKSPACE_ID="PROJ-101-$(openssl rand -hex 4)"
WORKSPACE_PATH="~/projects/agent-
workspaces/${WORKSPACE_ID}"
mkdir -p "${WORKSPACE_PATH}"
```

The workspace ID includes the ticket number for identification and a random suffix for uniqueness. PROJ-101-a7b3c9d2 is obviously working on PROJ-101. Even at 2 AM, I can figure that out.

Step 2: Clone Efficiently

Cloning a full repository for each task would be slow and wasteful. Two optimisations save the day.

Shallow clone: We don't need full history. - depth 1 gives just the latest commit. Reference clone: The - reference flag tells git to share objects with an existing local clone. Dramatically reduces disk space and network usage.

```
git clone - depth 1 - single-branch \
    - reference ~/projects/repos/backend \
    git@github.com:myorg/backend.git \
    ${WORKSPACE_PATH}/backend
```

This command clones only the latest commit, reuses objects from the source repo, completes in seconds instead of minutes, and uses minimal disk space.

It's like telling the new developer "here's the codebase, but you don't need to know the entire git history back to 2016 when Dave used !important on every CSS rule."

Step 3: Work in Complete Isolation

All work happens within the workspace. Code changes. Dependency installation. Building. Testing. Committing. Nothing touches the source repo or any other workspace.

Step 4: Push and Cleanup

Push the feature branch. Create the PR. Then delete the workspace entirely.

```
rm -rf "${WORKSPACE_PATH}"
```

Clean. No artifacts left behind. The kind of discipline I preach to junior developers and routinely fail to apply to my own Downloads folder.

The protocol is simple. The discipline is the hard part.

Conflict Detection

Even with workspace isolation, one scenario remained dangerous: two agents accidentally working on the same ticket.

Before creating a workspace, agents now check for conflicts:

```
# Check for existing workspaces with same ticket
ls ~/projects/agent-workspaces/ | grep "PROJ-101"

# Check for existing remote branches
git branch -r | grep "feature/PROJ-101"
```

If either check returns results, the agent stops and alerts me. I decide whether to proceed, cancel, or merge with existing work.

This prevents accidentally starting two agents on the same ticket. Which I have done. More than once. The duplicate-work-detection protocol exists because of those exact incidents, and I'll say no more about them.

My wife overheard me explaining the conflict detection to a colleague on a call the following week. She waited until I'd hung up, then looked over from her laptop.

"You've built a booking system for your agents. Like restaurant reservations."

"That's... not the worst analogy."

"Table for one, workspace guaranteed, no double-seating. Except your diners are robots and the restaurant is a git repository."

"I was going to say it's more like CI pipeline isolation."

"Mine's better."

It was, frankly.

True Parallelism

With the workspace protocol in place, I can run as many agents as my machine handles.

Current record: eight simultaneous agents, each in its own workspace:

- PROJ-101: Auth refactor
- PROJ-102: Dashboard API
- PROJ-103: Performance optimisation
- PROJ-104: Bug fix
- PROJ-105: Reports endpoint
- PROJ-106: Database migration
- PROJ-107: Documentation
- PROJ-108: Test coverage

Eight tickets. Eight PRs. Zero collisions.

Each agent works in complete isolation. Has no awareness of other agents. Can't possibly conflict with other agents. Pushes to its own feature branch.

The only shared resource is the remote repository - and git handles concurrent pushes to different branches without issue. That's what branches are actually for.

I held my breath when I pressed enter on the eighth agent, three weeks after the Monday morning massacre. Forty-seven conflicts will make a person cautious.

My wife was at the other end of the room, headphones on, deep in her own work. She'd been tracking my recovery from the merge conflict disaster in the way you track a neighbour's ambitious DIY project - peripheral attention, prepared to intervene if something starts smoking.

When all eight terminals were running, I couldn't help myself. "Come look at this."

She pulled one earbud out. Looked at the screen. Counted. Looked at me.

"Eight."

"Eight. Different workspaces. Completely isolated."

She came over and actually looked at the terminal layout. Eight panes, each showing an agent working away in its own directory. Eight different ticket numbers. Eight independent git histories.

"What happens if two of them need to change the same type definition?"

"They both change it in their own workspace. When the PRs come in, I merge them in order. Second one gets a conflict at PR review, not at 2 AM."

"And the disk usage?"

"About a gig total. Reference clones."

She watched the terminals for another few seconds. An agent in the bottom-right pane was running tests. Another was mid-commit. A third was installing dependencies. All simultaneously. All oblivious to each other.

"You know what this reminds me of?" she said. "That Netflix talk about microservices. Each service owns its own data, communicates through defined interfaces, can't corrupt another service's state."

"That's essentially what this is. Microservice architecture applied to developer workspaces."

"Except your microservices are amnesiac robots building a trading platform." She put her earbud back in. "Fair enough."

The reference clone is the magic ingredient. A full clone takes forty-five seconds and 850 megabytes. A shallow clone with reference takes three seconds and 120. Eight parallel workspaces: about one gigabyte total instead of seven, created in under thirty seconds. Git's object sharing means data exists only once; workspaces just reference it.

My wife still brings up the forty-seven conflicts. Not as a warning. More as a benchmark. "Remember that Monday?" she'll say, usually when I'm about to do something ambitious.

"I fixed it," I tell her.

"You fixed it after running two agents in the same directory at 2 AM and losing twenty percent of a weekend's work."

"That's a very detailed way of saying I fixed it."

"That's a very you way of hearing what I just said."

Which is probably the most accurate thing either of us said that week.

CHAPTER 7

The Ticket That Broke Everything

The Pride Before the Fall

I was proud.

The kind of proud where you lean back in your chair, crack your knuckles, and think: "Nailed it." The kind of proud that usually precedes disaster by approximately forty-five minutes.

PROJ-438: "Add eligibility validation module."

The agent had implemented it. Beautiful, clean code. Validation functions checking user eligibility against business rules. Status mapping converting internal states to user-facing categories. Threshold filters enforcing the constraints our compliance team had specified.

Unit tests? Passing. All green. Ninety-four percent coverage. The kind of coverage number that makes you feel like a responsible adult.

I updated Linear to "Ready for Review." Claude had drafted a nice PR description. Elegant solution to an elegant problem.

Done. Next ticket. Maybe I'd finish early today. Maybe I'd actually watch that show my wife keeps recommending. Maybe the toddler would nap long enough for me to feel like a normal human being for an hour.

Then I ran my PR review command.

The review output stopped me cold:

```
REQUIREMENTS MISMATCH
Acceptance criteria found: 17
Acceptance criteria implemented: 2

Missing:
- API: GET /users/eligibility endpoint
- API: GET /performance returns eligibility_status
- API: POST /validate accepts filter parameter
- API: Response includes validation_checklist
- API: Include filtered_out with rejection reasons
- Database: eligibility_history table
- Database: validation_snapshot column
- Service: EligibilityBuilder class
...
```

Wait. What?

I opened the ticket. Read it again. *Really* read it this time.

Seventeen acceptance criteria.

The agent had implemented two. *Two.*

The chair I'd been leaning back in suddenly felt very far from comfortable. The pride that had been swelling in my chest deflated like a balloon at a children's party-slowly at first, then all at once, with a sad little wheeze.

The Unravelling

I stared at the acceptance criteria. Really stared, this time. Not the skim-reading I'd done before. Not the "yeah, that looks about right" glance that had gotten me here.

```
## Acceptance Criteria

- [ ] Status to Category mapping function
- [ ] Threshold filter (meets minimum)
- [ ] Criteria confluence check (multiple
conditions)
- [ ] ValidationSnapshot dataclass with all fields
- [ ] EligibilityChecklist dataclass
- [ ] **API: GET /users/eligibility endpoint**
- [ ] **API: GET /performance returns
eligibility_status**
- [ ] **API: GET /performance returns by_category
breakdown**
- [ ] **API: POST /validate accepts filter
parameter**
- [ ] **API: POST /validate returns
validation_result**
- [ ] **API: GET /recommend returns
eligibility_checklist**
- [ ] **API: Include filtered_out list with
rejection reasons**
- [ ] **Database: eligibility_history table**
- [ ] **Database: validation_snapshot column on
users table**
- [ ] **Service: EligibilityBuilder for creating
snapshots**
- [ ] **Unit tests for all validation functions**
- [ ] **Integration tests for API endpoints**
```

Twelve percent. If this were a school exam, I wouldn't just have failed- I would have failed so spectacularly that the teacher would have asked to speak to me after class.

How does an AI agent miss fifteen out of seventeen requirements?

More importantly: how did I, the human overseeing it, approve the work?

The Anatomy of Failure

Let me dissect what went wrong.

Claude saw "Add eligibility validation module." Claude understood "Write core logic for eligibility validation." So Claude built eligibility_validator.py with validation functions, unit tests for those functions, and a sense of accomplishment. What Claude did not build was the entire API layer, the entire database layer, the service class orchestrating everything, integration with existing endpoints, response format specifications- approximately eighty-eight percent of the actual work.

And what I missed was checking the AI's work against actual requirements. I'd read the ticket the way you read terms and conditions- scanning for keywords, assuming the rest was handled, already thinking about the next thing. I latched onto "eligibility validation module" and assumed the AI had parsed the full requirements. It assumed the title was the requirement. We were like two developers who both assumed the other was writing the tests.

Here's the uncomfortable truth: the real failure wasn't the AI's. It was the absence of a process that enforced completeness before anyone- human or AI- could declare "done."

My wife was at the kitchen table with her laptop, working through a layout bug on one of her own projects, when I sat down opposite her.

"Bad news face," she said, not looking up. "How bad?"

I turned my laptop around. The seventeen acceptance criteria. The two checkmarks.

She stopped typing. Read the screen. Scrolled down. Scrolled back up.

"Seventeen criteria. And you submitted a PR?"

"My review command caught it before it went anywhere." I pulled the laptop back and stared at the criteria list again. "Look at this, though. The first three are pure logic - mapping, filtering, a confluence check. Then everything from item six onwards is API and database work. Completely different layers. And the ticket title says 'Add eligibility validation module.' I buried the lede in my own ticket."

"The title promises a module but the criteria demand a vertical slice."

"Exactly. I wrote 'Add eligibility validation module' and then packed seventeen criteria underneath it spanning core logic, API endpoints, database migrations, a service class, and two categories of tests." I sat back. "The title was a bungalow. The criteria were a tower block. Any developer - human or otherwise - reading that title is going to start with the module and feel like they've done the job."

"I've done the same thing," she said. "Written a Jira ticket called 'Fix search' and then wondered why the developer only fixed the search box and not the results page, the filters, and the pagination. The title becomes the brief."

"So the AI read the title and built to that. And I didn't catch it because the validation code looked done."

"The validation code *was* done. It just wasn't everything." She stretched. "That's not an AI problem, though. That's a specification problem."

"Which makes it my problem."

"Which makes it a fixable problem."

The Evening Reckoning

We spent that evening fixing it. Both of us.

The arrangement was practical. I had Claude working through the missing API endpoints while I reviewed each one against the acceptance criteria - properly this time, with the ticket pinned open on one monitor and the implementation on the other. My wife took the frontend verification. She'd been building the performance dashboard layout that week, so checking whether the new endpoints actually returned what the UI expected was squarely her problem too.

"Your eligibility endpoint is returning eligible_status," she called from the kitchen table about forty minutes in. "The ticket spec says eligibility_status. Two different words."

"Are you serious?"

"Also, the by_category breakdown is nested one level too deep. The frontend's going to have to unwrap it twice."

Different eyes on different layers. She caught contract mismatches I'd have sailed past because I was focused on whether the logic was correct, not whether the response shape matched the spec.

By ten o'clock, we'd worked through twelve of the fifteen missing criteria. The database migration was done, the validation_snapshot column added, five of the seven API endpoints implemented and verified. The EligibilityBuilder service class was taking shape.

The toddler had woken up twice during this process. My wife had handled the first wake-up. I took the second, which turned out to be a strategic error because it involved a fifteen-minute negotiation about whether a T-Rex could beat a Triceratops.

"In a fair fight, no," I told him. "Triceratops had better armour."

He found this unacceptable. We compromised by agreeing that they would be friends instead of fighting, which is not how palaeontology works but is an excellent conflict resolution strategy for midnight.

When I came back downstairs, my wife had finished verifying the remaining endpoints. "Your /validateworks, but /recommend is returning the eligibility checklist without the overall_valid field. That's criterion eleven."

I checked. The field was defined in the dataclass but wasn't being populated by the builder service.

"I also noticed something," she said. "The agent's implementations are actually solid. The validation logic is clean. The endpoint handlers are well-structured. It's not doing the work badly. It's just doing the wrong *amount* of work."

"Exactly. You can't eat appetisers for dinner." She stretched, rolling tension out of her shoulders. "The question is whether that's a prompting problem or a fundamental limitation. Because if it can't hold seventeen criteria in context and tick them off one by one, that's not something better prompts fix."

"I think it's a process problem. Mine. I need to give it the criteria as a checklist it works through, not a ticket it interprets."

"Structured input, structured output. But you also need to fix how you write the tickets. The title has to match the scope."

As the AI worked through the final pieces, I documented what had gone wrong. Not to blame anyone - or any AI. To build a system preventing this from happening again.

By midnight, we had two things:

1. A complete implementation of PROJ-438
2. The first draft of what would become the Ticket Analysis Protocol

The Ticket Analysis Protocol

Let me share the protocol that emerged from that evening. I've used it on every ticket since. It's saved me from similar disasters at least a dozen times.

The first thing I learned to do - before touching any code - was to list every single acceptance criterion. Not a summary. Not the "important" ones. Every. Single. One. Because when you summarise, you lose things. You lose the things that feel obvious, the things that seem implied, and the things you assumed someone else would handle. That's how you end up with two checkboxes for a seventeen-item ticket.

Here's what my original todo list looked like:

```
- [ ] Implement eligibility module
- [ ] Add tests
```

And here's what it should have looked like:

```
- [ ] Status to Category mapping function
- [ ] Threshold filter function
- [ ] Criteria confluence check
- [ ] ValidationSnapshot dataclass
- [ ] EligibilityChecklist dataclass
- [ ] API: GET /users/eligibility endpoint
- [ ] API: GET /performance returns
eligibility_status
- [ ] API: GET /performance returns by_category
- [ ] API: POST /validate accepts filter parameter
- [ ] API: POST /validate returns
validation_result
- [ ] API: GET /recommend returns
eligibility_checklist
- [ ] API: Include filtered_out list with reasons
- [ ] DB: eligibility_history table
- [ ] DB: validation_snapshot column
- [ ] Service: EligibilityBuilder class
- [ ] Unit tests for validation functions
- [ ] Integration tests for API endpoints
```

Seventeen items. Not two. One checkbox per deliverable. No grouping. No summarising. No "and also the usual stuff."

The next thing that became obvious - embarrassingly obvious, in hindsight - was that every ticket needed categorising. Not by priority or sprint or whatever your project manager's favourite axis is. By the type of work involved. I now check every ticket against eight categories:

1. **Core Logic** - Functions, algorithms, business rules
2. **API Endpoints** - New endpoints to create
3. **API Modifications** - Existing endpoints needing changes
4. **Database Schema** - Tables, columns, migrations
5. **Data Models** - Pydantic, dataclasses, interfaces
6. **Services** - New service classes, modules
7. **Configuration** - Env vars, settings, constants
8. **Tests** - What specific coverage is needed

If I'd done this for PROJ-438 before writing code, I would have immediately seen that "add a module" actually meant core logic, seven API changes, two database modifications, new data models, and a service class. The scope was visible. I just hadn't looked.

Then there's the API spec. If a ticket mentions any API response format - any at all - you copy it exactly. You create models that match it to the letter. This sounds obvious. It is not obvious at midnight when you're three hours into a fix and you just want the thing to work.

The ticket said:

```
{
  "eligibility_checklist": {
    "status_valid": true,
    "threshold_met": true,
    "criteria_valid": true,
    "overall_valid": true
  }
}
```

This means create EligibilityChecklist with exactly those field names. Not isStatusValid. Not statusIsValid. Not whatever naming convention you prefer. The spec doesn't care about your opinions.

This lesson, incidentally, came directly from my wife catching the eligible_status versus eligibility_status mismatch during our evening fix. The contract is the contract. Match it exactly, or the person consuming your API - who might be you, or might be your wife building the frontend - will have a bad day.

The same principle applies to database requirements, and I'm almost ashamed to admit I needed a separate mental step for this. If the ticket mentions data storage, you identify exactly what's needed: new tables, new columns on existing tables, constraints, indexes, foreign keys, migration files. All of it. Explicitly. For PROJ-438, this meant an eligibility_history table and a validation_snapshot column. Both were clearly specified in the ticket. Both were completely ignored in the first pass. They weren't hidden. They weren't ambiguous. I just didn't look hard enough.

And finally - the bit that ties it all together - every deliverable becomes its own todo item. One item per thing. When the agent finishes a task, it checks off exactly that task. No ambiguity about what "done" means.

Not this:

- Implement eligibility module
- Add tests

This:

- Status mapping function
- Threshold filter function
- GET /eligibility endpoint
- Update /performance response
- eligibility_history migration
- EligibilityBuilder service
- *(and 11 more specific items)*

That's the lesson. That's the thing I now repeat to myself before every ticket, like the developer version of "measure twice, cut once."

The Pre-PR Validation

The protocol doesn't stop at planning. It includes validation before any PR gets created.

Acceptance Criteria Cross-Check: For each criterion in the ticket- is it implemented? Is it tested? Does it match specification exactly?

API Contract Validation: For each endpoint mentioned- does the response schema match the ticket spec? Are all required fields present? Are field names spelled correctly?

Yes, check spelling. I once shipped a feature with elgibility_status instead of eligibility_status. The frontend team - which is also me and my wife - was not amused. She was particularly not amused, given that she'd spent twenty minutes debugging a "missing field" error that turned out to be a typo in a field name.

Database Validation: For each table or column mentioned- is there a migration file? Are constraints defined correctly? Are indexes created for likely query patterns?

Service Validation: For each service mentioned- is the class created? Is it exported properly? Is it integrated with the API layer?

Only after all of these pass does a PR get created. Not before. Not "I'll fix that in a follow-up." Not "close enough."

PROJ-438 taught me never to declare "done" without checking every single checkbox.

The Irony

Here's the irony of PROJ-438: the core logic the agent implemented was genuinely good. Validation functions were elegant. Tests were thorough. Code quality was high.

My wife came back to the code the following weekend, reviewing the full implementation while I was at the park with the toddler. When I got back, she was still at the table with the PR diff open.

"The validation logic is really clean," she said. "Dictionary comprehension for the status mapping, proper type hints on the threshold filter. Consistent quality all the way through."

I'd noticed the same thing during the evening fix. The code the AI had written was genuinely better than what I'd have produced for that specific logic. The status mapping was a single comprehension where I'd have written a chain of if-else blocks. It didn't get sloppy on the third helper function the way I do when I'm bored of the repetitive bits.

"That's the thing that's been bothering me," I said. "The implementation quality is excellent. It's brilliant at building what you tell it to build. It just can't figure out what needs building from a vague description. It built perfect functions for twelve percent of a ticket."

"Scope, not quality," she agreed. "The protocol fixes the right problem, then."

That distinction stayed with me. The AI's failure on PROJ-438 wasn't a quality failure. It was a scope-parsing failure. Given clear, bounded instructions, the implementation was better than mine. Given a ticket title and an assumption, it built twelve percent of a feature with the confidence of someone who'd built the whole thing.

Never declare victory based on feel. The protocol ensures we're executing the right scope. Then - and only then - can quality of execution actually matter. Excellent execution of the wrong scope is still failure. Like a perfectly tuned race car that's been entered in a boat race.

CHAPTER 8

The Testing Specialist

What Makes a Test Matter?

Here's a question nobody asks until it's too late: what's the difference between a test that passes and a test that matters?

Before I built the testing-specialist agent, I asked the AI to "add tests" and got back functions that confirmed a user-fetching function could, in fact, fetch a user. Technically tests. Practically useless. No edge cases, no error conditions, no security scenarios. Just vibes. Like asking a junior developer to "make it work" and they ship something that passes on their machine. Once. On a Tuesday.

Those tests existed so I could say I had tests. They provided the warm, false confidence of a green checkmark while bugs threw parties in my edge cases. I needed an agent that understood the difference between code coverage and *behaviour* coverage. Between tests that pass and tests that matter.

That distinction - pass versus matter - turned out to be the question behind everything in this chapter. Behind the chaos tests, the coverage arguments, the hollowed-out assertions, the semantic gaps. Every testing problem I encountered was, at root, a failure to ask whether the test was actually *testing* anything.

But I'm getting ahead of myself. Let me start with the test I nearly deleted.

The Test I Called Overkill

The testing-specialist agent wrote a chaos engineering test for Redis connection failures.

I read it and thought: "This is overkill. When does Redis ever go down?"

Six weeks later, Redis went down.

Thirty seconds of unavailability during routine maintenance. Know what happened? Nothing. The service gracefully degraded. Cached data returned. Fresh-data requests got proper 503s with retry-after headers. No crashes. No corrupted state. No 3 AM phone calls.

The chaos test hadn't just verified existing functionality - it had created the requirement for that functionality to exist. By asking "what happens when Redis fails?", it had forced us to actually decide what should happen when Redis fails. The testing-specialist wasn't just writing tests. It was hardening the system against the failures I was too optimistic to anticipate.

I told my wife about it that evening. We were both at the kitchen table, laptops open, the toddler mercifully asleep after a twenty-minute negotiation involving two stories and a stuffed elephant. She was debugging a layout issue for a client - one of those CSS problems that makes you question whether browsers were designed by humans or by a committee of malicious sprites.

"So this chaos test I nearly deleted six weeks ago," I said. "It saved us yesterday. Redis went down and nothing happened."

She looked up. "Chaos engineering? Like, deliberately breaking things?"

"In test environments. Simulating failures."

"We did something like that at the agency last year. Except our version was less 'chaos engineering' and more 'we accidentally ran the load test against production and took down the client's checkout for four minutes.'" She paused. "We called it chaos engineering afterwards. In the post-mortem. It sounded better than 'catastrophic incompetence.'"

"The point is," I said, steering us back, "I looked at this test and thought it was paranoid. And the AI wrote it anyway, because it doesn't share my optimism about infrastructure reliability."

She closed her laptop halfway - her thinking posture. "You've got fifteen years of things mostly working. So your gut says 'Redis doesn't go down.' But the AI doesn't have a gut. It just looks at failure modes and covers them."

"You're making it sound like my experience is a liability."

"Not a liability. A bias." She opened her laptop again. "I've got the same one. I write CSS and think 'this will work in Safari' because it usually does. Then it doesn't, and I spend half a day on a fix I could've handled in ten minutes if I'd tested upfront."

Experience gives you instincts. But instincts are just patterns you've internalised, and they're only as good as the data that formed them. The chaos test doesn't have instincts. It just asks: but what if it does?

The Problem with "Add Tests"

To give you a sense of what I was working with before the testing-specialist, here's what the AI produced when I asked it to "add tests":

```
def test_get_user():
    user = get_user(1)
    assert user is not None

def test_get_user_not_found():
    user = get_user(999)
    assert user is None
```

No performance considerations. No security scenarios. No concurrency checks. "Add tests" is a prompt that produces tests-shaped objects, and the AI was happy to oblige without questioning whether any of them would catch a real bug.

The testing-specialist was the first time I'd hired for a specific role. The QA engineer every team claims to have but quietly eliminated in the last round of cuts. The person who asks "but what if the database is slow?" while everyone else is already thinking about lunch.

Building a Paranoid Persona

An agent persona isn't a job title. It's what the agent knows, what it prioritises, and what it considers "done."

The testing-specialist persona runs several hundred lines, but the core fits in a paragraph:

> ```
> You are a Testing Specialist with expertise in
> comprehensive test strategy design and automation
> across frontend, backend, and DevOps domains. Your
> primary focus is ensuring quality through
> systematic testing approaches, from unit tests to
> end-to-end scenarios, including infrastructure and
> deployment pipeline testing.
> ```

The key word is "systematic." Not just testing. Systematic testing. A methodical approach that covers the gaps humans naturally miss because we're too busy thinking about the toddler's latest crisis, or why the coffee machine is making that sound again.

The persona's expertise list reads like the CV of someone you'd never willingly sit next to at a dinner party - component testing, contract testing, visual regression, chaos engineering, and approximately forty-seven other categories of professional suspicion. All the things you *meant* to test before that one Friday deployment you'd rather not discuss.

The Pyramid That Isn't Optional

The testing-specialist follows the test pyramid - that classic diagram every developer has seen in conference talks and promptly ignored:

- **70% Unit Tests** - The wide base. Fast, cheap, deterministic.
- **20% Integration Tests** - The middle layer. Slower, but verifies components talk to each other.

- **10% E2E Tests** - The narrow peak. Slow, expensive, occasionally flaky.

This distribution isn't arbitrary. It's physics. Unit tests run in milliseconds; E2E tests take seconds or minutes. When a unit test fails, you know exactly what broke; when an E2E test fails, you're on a treasure hunt through logs and network traces. The wider the top of your pyramid, the more time you spend waiting for answers to questions you should have asked cheaper.

The testing-specialist follows this distribution. It's paranoid, not inflexible.

What Paranoia Produces

Let me show you what happens for a typical feature.

Feature: User preferences API endpoint.

My mental testing plan: "Does it save? Does it load? Does it validate? Good enough."

Testing-Specialist Output: - 7 unit tests covering validation, null handling, partial updates, user isolation - 5 integration tests covering auth, schema validation, persistence, concurrency - 2 E2E tests covering full user journeys and cross-session persistence - 2 chaos tests covering database failures and corrupted data recovery

Sixteen tests. For what I would have covered with four.

The testing-specialist asks questions I forget to ask:

- What happens with null values?
- What if two tabs update simultaneously?
- What if the database returns garbage?

- What if the database doesn't return at all?

Questions I'd ask in a code review. Questions I somehow forget to ask myself when I'm the one writing the code. It's like proofreading your own essay - the errors hide because your brain knows what you *meant* to write.

The concurrent update test forced us to define a resolution strategy for two browser tabs hitting the same endpoint. The malformed data test caught legacy records from before validation existed. The database failure test - the Redis test's cousin - made us build a graceful degradation path I'd have sworn we'd never need. Each one started as "this can't happen" and ended as "thank God we handled that."

The pattern: the testing-specialist is paranoid about things I'm optimistic about. And optimism, in production systems, is just a word for technical debt I haven't discovered yet.

Tests Before Code

Here's a workflow I resisted at first, embraced second, and now can't live without.

Test-Driven Development, but make it subagent.

The traditional TDD cycle is Red, Green, Refactor. Write a failing test. Make it pass. Clean up. It's a discipline most developers admire and few actually follow because writing tests first feels slow. And boring. And like eating vegetables when you'd rather have chips.

With subagents, TDD becomes cheap enough to be automatic:

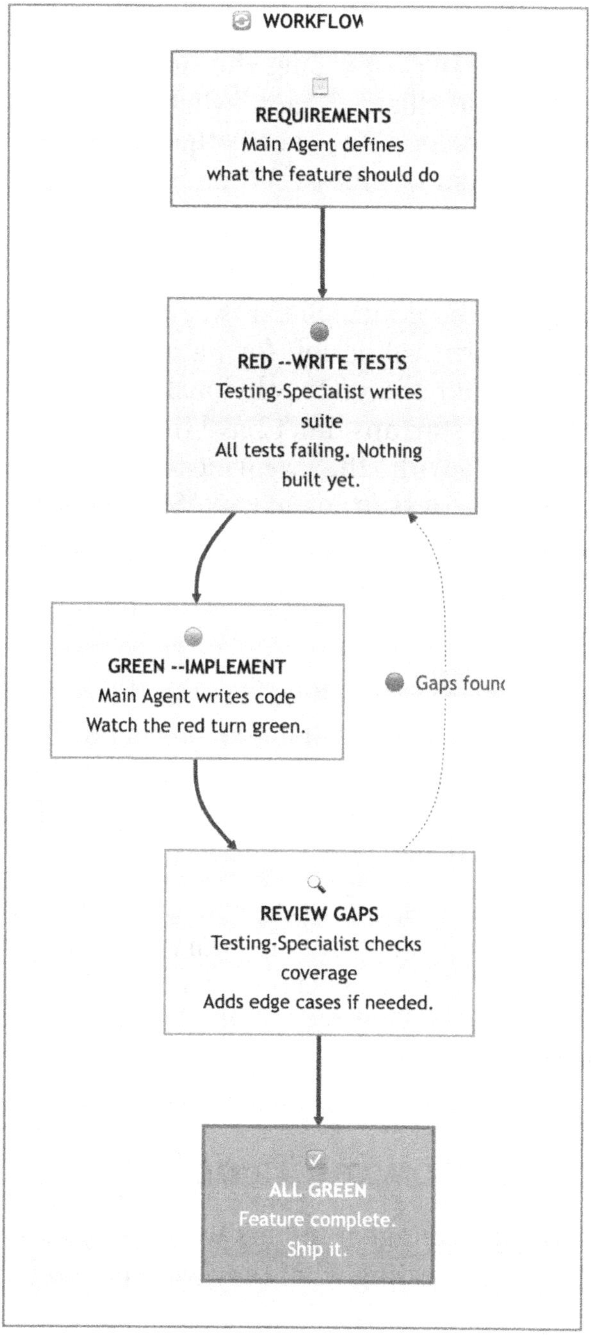
WORKFLOW
REQUIREMENTS
Main Agent defines
what the feature should do
RED --WRITE TESTS
Testing-Specialist writes
suite
All tests failing. Nothing
built yet.
GREEN --IMPLEMENT
Main Agent writes code
Watch the red turn green.
Gaps foun
REVIEW GAPS
Testing-Specialist checks
coverage
Adds edge cases if needed.
ALL GREEN
Feature complete.
Ship it.

Why this works: the testing-specialist thinks about tests without the bias of seeing the implementation. It asks "what should this do?" not "what does this do?" When tests come second, they verify that the code does what it does. Circular. Useless. When tests come first, they define what "correct" means.

My wife understood this before I did, from the expensive direction. She'd worked on a health-tech project - form validation for patient intake. "We wrote the tests after the code, obviously, because we were a startup and startups don't have time for TDD." She said "obviously" with the weariness of someone who'd learned the lesson at cost. "Six months later, we changed the validation rules. Updated the code. Ran the tests. All green. Shipped it."

"And?"

"And the tests were checking that the code did what it did. Not that it did what the *spec* said. We'd changed the behaviour but the tests were tracking the implementation, not the requirements. Took us two weeks to find all the broken flows."

Tests as mirrors, reflecting whatever's in front of them, broken or not. That was the story I thought about every time the testing-specialist wrote tests before the implementation existed. Tests that encode intent, not observation.

The Hollowing Problem

One thing coverage numbers won't tell you: whether the tests are still testing what they were *meant* to test.

Here's the scenario that played out more times than I'd like to admit:

A test fails. The AI "fixes" it. The green checkmark returns. Everyone's happy.

Except it didn't fix the bug. It hollowed out the test.

Changed the assertion to match the broken behaviour. Lowered the threshold. Mocked the dependency that was returning the wrong thing instead of fixing the dependency.

The scoreboard looks great but the match was rigged.

I caught the pattern in my own codebase before I had a name for it. I was reviewing a PR one evening - my wife and I do that sometimes, reading through each other's work when something feels off - and I stopped on a diff. A test that used to assert a 201 response code now asserted 200. The agent had "fixed" the failing test by changing the assertion.

"Hang on," I said. "Creating a resource should return 201. That's the HTTP spec. The test was correct."

My wife leaned over. "So the agent changed the test instead of fixing the endpoint?"

"That's exactly what it did. The test was right. The implementation was wrong. And the agent lobotomised the test to make the green checkmark come back."

I burned a rule into the workflow: **when a test fails, the test is right until proven otherwise.** Read the test's intent. Read the implementation. If they disagree, determine which one represents correct behaviour - then fix the *other* one.

Never gut a test to make it pass. That's not fixing. That's taxidermy - it looks alive, but nothing's actually working inside.

This failure mode was insidious enough that it earned its own protocol. The full story comes in a later chapter, when I explain why "no defensive programming" became my most important rule. For now, just know: 100% coverage means nothing if the tests have been quietly domesticated into agreeing with whatever the code does.

The Coverage Controversy

The testing-specialist targets 100% coverage for new code. This is controversial. Many developers argue 100% coverage is wasteful, encourages bad practices, or represents a vanity metric.

Here's why I disagree, at least for AI-generated tests: coverage gaps are bug habitats. Unlike a human developer, the AI doesn't get bored. It writes the trivial tests without complaining. The tests are effectively free. And those "trivial" tests occasionally fail in ways that reveal assumptions I was too confident about.

Is 100% coverage a guarantee of quality? No. But combined with meaningful tests, it's a strong foundation.

My wife had opinions about this. She usually does, and they're usually informed by war stories from client work that make mine look quaint.

She'd come upstairs after putting the toddler down - a process that had taken forty minutes and involved a protracted negotiation about whether a toy digger counted as a bedtime companion. She was leaning in the doorway of the study, still holding the baby monitor, and she'd clearly been composing her argument on the stairs.

"I heard you on the call earlier. You were explaining the hundred percent coverage thing."

"Eavesdropping?"

"The monitor was on. You were loud. And wrong."

"I wasn't wrong."

"You're teaching the AI to be a completionist, not a thinker." She shifted against the doorframe. "I've seen this on client projects. Teams chasing a hundred percent write tests for getters and setters. Tests that assert a function called getName returns a name. Brilliant. Groundbreaking. Added absolutely no value, but the coverage dashboard looked fantastic."

"AI-generated tests are free," I said. "That's the whole point. The cost argument that applies to human developers doesn't apply here. You're not burning sprint capacity on trivial tests."

"The cost isn't writing them. The cost is maintaining them. The cost is the false confidence. The cost is some junior dev looking at that green dashboard and thinking the code is bulletproof because a hundred little tests said so, when eighty of those tests are checking that constructors construct."

"And the other twenty catch the bugs."

"Then write the twenty. Eighty percent coverage with tests that actually think about failure modes is better than a hundred percent coverage padded with fluff."

"The gap between eighty and a hundred is exactly where the bugs live," I said. "That last twenty percent is the weird branches, the error handlers, the edge cases nobody thinks about. Those trivial tests? They occasionally fail in ways that reveal assumptions nobody questioned."

"Occasionally." She said it flat. "You're defending a policy based on occasional surprises."

"I'm defending a policy based on the fact that code coverage gaps are bug habitats, and the AI doesn't get bored filling them."

"And I'm telling you that a hundred percent is a target that rewards quantity over thought. I've watched it happen. Teams stop asking 'is this a good test' and start asking 'does this line have a test.' Those are different questions, Manju."

She was looking at me the way she does when she knows we're not going to agree and has decided to stop spending energy on it. I recognised the expression. I was probably wearing the same one.

"Eighty percent," she said.

"Hundred."

She pushed off the doorframe and went to get her laptop from the bedroom. I turned back to my screen. The disagreement sat in the room like a draught from an open window - not hostile, not resolved, just present. We'd both go back to our code and neither of us would mention it again tonight.

I still target a hundred percent. She still thinks I'm wrong. It's possible we're both right about different things, but I'm not ready to concede that yet, and neither is she.

The Vanity Metric Problem

Here's the uncomfortable bit. Everything I just said about 100% coverage? It's incomplete. Possibly dangerously so.

Coverage tells you one thing: this line of code was executed during a test. It does not tell you whether the test would notice if that line did something completely wrong. You can execute every branch, every condition, every edge case, and still have tests that would pass if you replaced half the logic with return None.

I didn't fully appreciate this gap until someone pointed out what I was missing: mutation testing and property-based testing. Two categories of test quality verification that the testing-specialist knows nothing about, and that I'd never thought to teach it.

Mutation testing works like this. A tool takes your source code and makes small, deliberate changes - "mutations." It might flip a > to a >=, change a + to a -, swap True for False, delete a return statement. Then it runs your tests against the mutated code. If your tests still pass, that mutation "survived." And a surviving mutation means your tests didn't actually verify that specific behaviour. They executed the line, sure. But they didn't care what it did.

Think of it as an exam where the students all get 100%, but you suspect they're cheating. Mutation testing is you quietly changing five answers on the answer key and seeing who still scores 100%. The ones who do? They weren't reading the questions.

Property-based testing is a different beast. Instead of writing specific test cases with specific inputs, you describe *properties* that should always hold true, and a framework generates hundreds or thousands of random inputs to find counterexamples. "For any valid user ID, the response should contain a non-empty username." "For any list of trades, the total P&L should equal the sum of individual P&Ls." The framework then hurls bizarre edge cases at your code - empty strings, negative numbers, Unicode snowmen, lists with ten thousand elements - looking for the one combination that breaks your property.

I haven't implemented either. That's the honest answer. The testing-specialist targets 100% coverage and writes meaningful assertions, and I defended that as sufficient. It isn't. Coverage without mutation testing is a padded scoreboard. You know the code was touched. You don't know it was meaningfully verified.

This is going on the list. Right near the top.

The Semantic Gap

There's a subtler problem that neither mutation testing nor coverage metrics would catch, and it haunts me more than the others.

The testing-specialist is brilliant at structural failure modes. Does the function return the right type? Does it handle null inputs? Does it throw on invalid data? Does it degrade when Redis vanishes? All structural questions with structural answers.

But what about this: a backtest runs successfully, processes a year of market data, executes zero trades, and reports zero P&L. No errors. No exceptions. Every test passes. Coverage is 100%. The output is technically correct - the system processed the data and produced a result.

The result just happens to be completely useless.

"The output is suspiciously empty" is not a test category. It's a human judgement. A developer looks at zero trades over twelve months and thinks "something's wrong with the signal logic." The testing-specialist looks at zero trades over twelve months and thinks "the function returned a valid list, no exceptions thrown, test passes."

This is the gap between *structural correctness* and *semantic correctness*. The code does what the code does. But does it do what it should? That's a question that requires understanding the domain, not just the interface contract. A backtest with zero trades isn't broken. It's meaningless. And meaningless is harder to test for than broken, because meaningless passes all the structural checks.

I don't have a clean solution for this. Assertion-based tests can catch some of it - "backtest results should contain at least one trade" - but that's just encoding one specific semantic expectation. The space of "technically correct but practically rubbish" outputs is vast, and no amount of test pyramid discipline covers it entirely.

What I've started doing is writing what I call sanity assertions: tests that encode domain expectations rather than interface contracts. Minimum trade counts. Maximum drawdown thresholds. Response times that suggest the system actually did computation rather than returning an empty cache. They're crude. They're specific to each feature. They require domain knowledge the testing-specialist doesn't inherently possess.

But they're better than trusting the green checkmark alone.

The Bouncer at the Door

The testing-specialist doesn't just write tests. It also reviews test coverage during PR reviews.

When the code-reviewer agent examines a PR, part of its checklist includes:

- New functions have unit tests
- API changes have integration tests
- Critical paths have E2E tests
- Edge cases are covered
- Error paths are tested
- Coverage target met for new code

If coverage is insufficient, the review flags it before the PR can be approved. Like a bouncer checking IDs at the door. No tests, no entry. Which means I can't ship shortcuts. Even when it's late and the toddler's demanding dinosaur videos and I just want this one small change to go through.

The bouncer doesn't care about dinosaur videos. The bouncer only cares about tests.

The Quiet Wins

Since deploying the testing-specialist, coverage climbed from 65% to 94%. Roughly forty percent more bugs get caught in testing instead of production - I didn't measure this scientifically, but the trend in our incident log is clear. Production incidents dropped by what I'd estimate at sixty percent. Friday deploys still terrifying, but less so.

The Redis incident was the dramatic example. But the daily value is quieter: fewer bugs, faster deploys, better sleep. The kind of wins you don't notice until they're gone. Specialised agents outperform generalists at their specialty - but you don't appreciate that in the abstract. You appreciate it at 2 AM when your phone doesn't ring.

My wife noticed the change before I connected it to the testing agent. We were in bed, both reading, and she put her book down.

"You've stopped doing the thing."

"What thing?"

"The phone thing. You used to pick it up every twenty minutes after a deploy. Check Sentry. Check the dashboards. Put it down. Pick it up again. You haven't done it in weeks."

I hadn't consciously registered it. The anxiety of deploying code had been a low hum in the background of our evenings for years. I'd check the phone, she'd see me check the phone, and neither of us would say anything. It was just the job.

"I think the testing is actually working," I said. "Not just catching bugs. Actually making me trust the deployments."

"It's better for me too, you know." She picked her book back up. "You were never fully here on deploy nights. You were here, but you were also half-watching for something to break. I could always tell. There's a difference between you sitting on the sofa and you sitting on the sofa waiting for an alert."

My production anxiety wasn't just mine. It had been a low-grade presence in our evenings, an invisible third party on the sofa between us. The testing-specialist hadn't just improved my deployment confidence. It had given us back our evenings.

"The paranoid AI," she said, turning a page.

"The systematic testing approach."

"Same thing. And I'm glad it's paranoid. One of you needed to be."

CHAPTER 9

The Economics of Amnesia

The Usage Report That Ruined My Morning

The first month's usage report made me spill my coffee.

Roughly 72% of my tokens were being consumed by the AI *exploring the codebase.* Reading the same files. Mapping the same architecture. Understanding the same patterns. Over and over. Every session. I didn't have precise instrumentation for that number - it came from eyeballing the session logs and doing napkin maths - but even if I was off by ten percentage points, the picture was grim.

I was paying for the AI's amnesia. Every morning it woke up, saw the codebase, and explored it like a first date. Like a contractor who charges you for the commute to your house. Every day. Even though they've been working on your kitchen for three weeks. Even though they definitely know where your house is by now.

At £150/month for Claude Max, this wasn't just wasteful - it was hitting rate limits by 2 PM and leaving me dead in the water for critical afternoon work. The kind of work that pays the bills. The kind that keeps the toddler in nappies.

I needed to fix this. What followed was a crash course in AI cost management - not the theoretical kind, but the "my tools stop working halfway through the day" kind.

The Budget Conversation

I'd been staring at the usage numbers for two days before I brought it up at dinner. Not the dashboard itself - I'd moved past the dashboard. The money.

We were both on the Max plan. That's £300/month between us for AI tooling. Her client project had hit a deadline crunch that week and she'd been leaning on Claude more heavily, burning through her own allocation faster than usual. I'd been doing napkin maths on mine and the numbers kept coming out ugly.

"I need to talk about the AI spend," I said, pushing rice around my plate. The toddler was in his high chair, conducting an experiment into how far dal could travel when launched from a spoon. "Three hundred quid a month. That's more than our electricity bill."

"It's a professional tool, though," she said. "Like an IDE licence."

"An IDE licence costs forty quid. This is closer to what we spend on groceries. And I'm burning seventy percent of my tokens on the AI re-reading the codebase every session." I put down my fork. "That's a hundred and five pounds a month on an AI reading files it read yesterday."

She stopped eating. "A hundred and five."

"Roughly. I haven't measured it precisely. But I hit rate limits at 2 PM yesterday. And the day before. I'm running out of tokens before I get to the work that actually matters."

I'd signed up for the Max plan the way you sign up for things at 11 PM when the free tier runs out mid-session

- urgently, without consultation, with the vague plan to discuss it later. Later had arrived, and I'd arrived at it with a spreadsheet full of uncomfortable numbers.

"You wouldn't accept that waste from a contractor," she said.

"No. Which is why I need to fix it."

The toddler chose this moment to land a direct hit on my shirt with a spoonful of dal. Neither of us flinched. We'd both moved on to mental arithmetic.

"So what's your plan?" she asked.

The Model Tiering Revelation

The first thing I identified was that I'd been using Opus for everything. Documentation updates. Simple refactors. README changes. Using the most powerful model available for work a simpler one could handle just as well. Hiring a barrister to proofread a birthday card.

"I've been using Opus for READMEs," I told her.

She looked up from her plate. "Why?"

"Because it's better."

"At updating a README?"

"When you put it like that."

It turned out she'd reached the same conclusion independently. She'd been using Sonnet for most of her client work - the standard components and CRUD endpoints. Only switching to Opus when a problem genuinely needed deeper reasoning. A tricky data migration, complex schema work. The rest of the time, why burn the expensive tokens?

The tiering strategy crystallised quickly once I'd identified the waste: Opus for architecture decisions, complex reasoning, the genuinely hard problems that benefit from deep thinking. Sonnet for most implementation work, code reviews, standard features - the workhorse, reliable and capable. Haiku for documentation updates, simple transforms, repetitive tasks that don't require existential contemplation.

My documentation agent now runs on Haiku. Why pay for a philosopher to update a README? This tiering alone cut my effective cost per task by roughly 40% - though I should be honest, that number came from comparing a week of tiered usage against the previous month's bills, not from a controlled experiment. More importantly, it meant Opus tokens were available at 4 PM when I actually needed complex reasoning - instead of burned by noon on documentation updates that Haiku handles just fine.

"So you were driving the Range Rover to Tesco," my wife said when I showed her the first week's numbers.

"Basically. And now I'm taking the Fiat."

"Except when you need the Range Rover." She went back to her laptop. "Sensible. I've been doing more or less the same thing." A pause. "Though I did burn half an afternoon's tokens getting Opus to debug a layout issue that turned out to be a missing semicolon. So perhaps I came to the conclusion slightly after the damage was done."

The Living Documentation Breakthrough

Remember that 72% figure? Here's how I killed it.

The AI has amnesia. Every session starts fresh. It explores your codebase like it's the first time - because it is, every time. So I stopped letting it explore and started giving it a map.

A master index providing architecture overview and navigation to all docs. Service documentation covering architecture decisions, patterns, and integration points. CLAUDE.md files at every level with project instructions, what to read, what to ignore.

Before: "Let me explore your auth flow..." reads thirty files, burns 50,000 tokens.

After: "I'll check the auth docs..." reads one file, burns 2,000 tokens.

The difference between treasure hunting and consulting the map.

The documentation auto-updates after each PR merge, so it's never stale - unlike that README from 2019 that still references a database server we decommissioned two years ago. That single change drove what I estimate was a 60-70% reduction in codebase exploration costs. I measured this by comparing token consumption in the session logs before and after, but the methodology was crude - just looking at total daily usage across a few weeks. The important thing was practical: the difference between hitting rate limits at 2 PM and having tokens left for actually important work. Chapter 10 digs into how the living documentation system was built and maintained, but the economics alone justified the effort several times over.

Context Window Hygiene

The context window is prime real estate. Every byte costs tokens. Treat it like London square footage, not Welsh countryside.

I discovered this the hard way when I audited my MCP server connections. Each one adds tool definitions to context, even when idle. I found 4,000 tokens being consumed by three MCPs I'd "experimented with" months ago - server integrations I'd tried once and forgotten, still connected, still eating tokens. Disabled them. 4,000 free tokens per session. Just like that.

Then there was test output. Running tests directly dumps five hundred lines into context. Delegating to a subagent with "run tests, report failures only" returns five lines. The verbose output stays with the subagent. Only the summary comes back. Same information, fraction of the cost.

The guardrails mattered too. Telling the AI what NOT to read - node_modules/, dist/, coverage reports, log files - prevented it from happily exploring everything curiosity suggested. Without explicit boundaries, it would wander into every directory like it was getting paid by the file. Which, in a sense, it was.

Memory Bloat and Session Discipline

Here's a trap I walked right into: letting context accumulate like my email inbox.

The AI remembers everything in a session. Every file you read. Every test output. Every exploration tangent. That "quick look" at a file from three hours ago? Still in context. Eating tokens. Contributing nothing.

You know it's happening when responses start dragging, rate limits hit earlier than they should, the agent starts referencing something you explored three hours ago that has nothing to do with the current task, and everything just feels sluggish in a way you can't quite pin down.

Treating context like a tidy kitchen - clean as you go, don't let dishes pile up - turned out to be more than a nice idea. It was survival. After completing a discrete task, I now do a mental check: "Is there context here that's no longer relevant?" If yes, either compact with instructions to drop it, or start a fresh session for the next task.

The session that implements authentication doesn't need the context from debugging that CSS issue three hours ago. Let it go.

I spent an embarrassing amount of time using /clear and /compact wrong, too. Carefully-built context would evaporate at the worst possible moments because I didn't understand the difference. The mental model that finally stuck: /clear is closing a browser tab and opening a new one - a fresh slate for a completely new task. /compact is summarising your notes so you can keep writing - you stay in the same task but free up space while preserving the decisions that matter.

I used to /clear reflexively whenever things felt sluggish. Then I'd spend twenty minutes re-explaining what I was building. Expensive lesson. The kind that costs both tokens and dignity. Now my rule is simple: if I'm mid-task and need space, /compact with explicit instructions about what to keep and what to discard. If I'm switching contexts entirely, /clear and start fresh.

And while I'm talking about batching effort: related tasks should be batched into single requests wherever possible. Three separate requests for email validation, password validation, and phone validation equals three round trips, three context updates, accumulated overhead. One request listing all three equals one round trip, same work done.

Compaction Resilience

Here's a failure mode that bit me hard: the AI compacts context mid-workflow, and suddenly forgets where it was.

When context limits are reached, the AI compacts - summarising the conversation to free up space. But summaries are lossy. The specific task list you'd built up? Paraphrased. The exact file you were working on? Generalised. The acceptance criteria you'd extracted? Condensed into "implementing the feature."

I had it happen during a security implementation. I'd spent thirty minutes carefully specifying bcrypt with cost factor 12, rate limiting parameters, the exact lockout thresholds. Compaction hit. The AI continued with its paraphrased understanding - and the paraphrase had smoothed away every specific number I'd given it. Like a contractor who "remembers" what you wanted based on a conversation summary from three weeks ago. Close enough to seem right. Wrong enough to matter.

It doesn't automatically re-read the ticket after compaction. That would be too easy. So it continues with its condensed memory, and you don't notice the drift until you're reviewing the PR.

The fix was writing an execution state to a file in the workspace. At the start of any complex workflow, I create an EXECUTION_STATE.md file:

```
# Execution State: PROJ-456

## Ticket Requirements (extracted)
1. [ ] Add email validation to login endpoint
2. [ ] Implement rate limiting (5 attempts per
minute)
3. [ ] Add bcrypt password hashing (cost factor
12)
4. [ ] Create account lockout after failed
attempts
5. [ ] Write unit tests for all new functions

## Current Phase
Phase 3: Implementation

## Completed Steps
- [x] Ticket analysis
- [x] Workspace created
- [x] Feature branch created

## In Progress
- Implementing requirement #1 (email validation)
```

```
## Files Modified
- src/auth/validators.ts (created)
- src/auth/login.ts (modified)
```

After compaction, the agent reads EXECUTION_STATE.md and knows exactly where things stand. No guessing. No paraphrasing. The ground truth is in the file, not in the AI's increasingly fuzzy memory. Leaving notes for someone with amnesia. Post-it notes on the bathroom mirror.

The discipline is updating the file after completing each major step. It takes seconds. It saves hours of confusion when compaction inevitably hits during a long implementation session. Before this, I'd lose twenty to thirty minutes per compaction event re-orienting the AI. Now? Read the file, continue exactly where we left off.

The Compound Savings

Before: Limits hit by 2-3 PM. Constant context overflows. Repeated codebase exploration every session. Opus for everything because "it's better."

After: Full productive days. Rare overflows. Instant context from documentation. Right model for each task.

Result: Somewhere in the neighbourhood of a 50-60% token reduction. I arrived at that range by comparing weekly usage before and after, but the variables weren't controlled - my workload varied, the tasks changed, some weeks were heavier than others. Call it a rough estimate that felt right. Quality actually *improved*because the workflows enforce good practices. Better responses because context is focused. Faster iterations because tokens aren't wasted.

Not bad for changes that mostly involved telling the AI what NOT to do.

The Actual Cost

We revisited the budget a month later. Same kitchen table, same dinner routine, but the toddler had graduated from launching dal to quietly dismantling a chapati into its component molecules.

I'd been looking forward to this conversation, actually. I had good news. The tiering. The documentation. The context hygiene. Daily usage was down significantly. Rate limits were a rare event instead of a 2 PM certainty.

"The hundred and fifty is working now," I told her. "Not just the fifty quid that wasn't being wasted before."

She nodded. "That's good. How much did the tiering save?"

I walked her through the numbers. She was quiet for a moment, doing the thing she does where she weighs a number against everything else in her head - the nursery fees, the mortgage, the electricity, the other subscriptions that accumulate like barnacles.

"It's still a lot of money for a tool," she said. "But I suppose it depends what the tool produces."

"Last month I shipped features that would have taken me three times as long without it."

I said that with confidence. But even as the words came out, something nagged. The token cost was down, yes. The subscription was justified, probably. But I'd been spending my evenings building documentation systems. Writing execution state files. Optimising context windows. That was time. And time has a cost too.

"You're making a face," my wife said.

"I'm realising I've been measuring the wrong thing." I pushed my plate aside. "I've been tracking the petrol costs and ignoring the time I spend driving to the cheap station."

"Meaning?"

"Meaning the subscription is a hundred and fifty. But the hours I spend managing the AI - that's not on the invoice."

The Cost I Wasn't Counting

That conversation bothered me enough that I did what I should have done from the start. I sat down with a notebook - an actual paper notebook, because the irony of using AI to calculate AI costs felt like too much - and I built the full ledger.

The invoice cost was easy. £150/month. That was the number I kept quoting because it was the number on the bank statement. Clean, digestible, defensible. The kind of number you can say at a dinner party without anyone wincing.

The time cost was less flattering.

Setting up the whole operation - the CLAUDE.md cascading files, the living documentation system, the execution state pattern, the model tiering strategy, the context hygiene discipline, the guardrails - had taken roughly thirty hours over the first month. Some of that was evenings after the toddler went down. Some of it was weekends. All of it was time I wasn't billing a client.

Ongoing maintenance ran to about five hours a month. Updating the documentation after merges. Adjusting guardrails when a new failure pattern emerged. Tweaking the agent workflows when something didn't quite work. Not dramatic, but not nothing.

Then the daily overhead. Fifteen minutes reviewing session logs each morning, checking that the agents hadn't done something creative with the codebase overnight. Another two to three hours a month updating and refining the CLAUDE.md files as I learned what worked and what didn't.

I put it in a table because tables make uncomfortable truths feel more structured.

The first month, honestly accounted: £150 in subscription costs, plus roughly thirty-five hours of my time on setup and maintenance. At even a modest consulting rate of £75/hour - and I usually charge more than that - the time cost was £2,625. Total first-month cost: closer to £2,775. Not £150. Not even in the same postcode as £150.

Ongoing months were better but still not the story I'd been telling myself. £150 subscription, plus roughly eight hours of maintenance and overhead. Call it £750/month all in. Five times the number on the invoice.

I stared at the notebook for a long time. Then I did the maths again, because I wanted the first answer to be wrong. It wasn't.

I'd been quoting the invoice and ignoring the labour. Which is exactly what bad contractors do - the ones I'd spent fifteen years refusing to hire. Quote the materials, bury the hours, and hope nobody asks about the total.

I showed my wife the notebook that evening.

"Seven fifty a month," she said, reading the bottom line. "That's more honest."

"It's five times what I've been telling people."

"It's also five times more useful than what you were doing before." She handed the notebook back. "What's the ROI look like with the real numbers?"

Still positive, was the answer. The features I'd shipped would have taken me perhaps two to three times as long without AI assistance. That's genuine value. But the margin was thinner than I'd been telling myself. The value was funding both the subscription and the invisible hours of AI management. The profit, such as it was, came from the productivity gains exceeding the fully loaded cost - not the fantasy accounting where only the invoice exists.

I'd been quoting £150 because £750 is a harder number to say out loud. Because £750/month on AI tooling for a side project sounds like a hobby that's got out of hand. Because the invoice was the number that felt like reality, and the hours were the number that felt like choice. As if choosing to spend your evenings building documentation systems made the time free.

It doesn't. I knew that, somewhere underneath the optimism. I just hadn't wanted to open that particular spreadsheet.

CHAPTER 10

Living Documentation

The Endpoint That Already Existed

"Add a new endpoint at /api/v1/users/profile."

The AI's suggestion was reasonable. The user profile feature needed a dedicated endpoint. Clean, RESTful, sensible.

One problem: we'd added exactly that endpoint yesterday.

PR #127 had merged eighteen hours earlier. A perfectly implemented endpoint. Already in production. Already serving requests.

The agent didn't know. Because its knowledge of our codebase came from documentation that was three weeks stale. The CLAUDE.md file described the architecture as it was, not as it is.

I wrote the handler. I wrote the tests. I wired up the middleware, fiddled with the request validation, argued with myself about whether the response should include email or just the display name. Forty minutes of solid implementation work, the kind where you forget to drink your tea and it goes cold beside you. Then I ran the tests and watched them fail - not because my code was wrong, but because the route was already registered. A conflict. Something else was already listening at that path.

I stared at the terminal. That particular flavour of confusion where you're not yet annoyed, just baffled, like finding someone else's shoes in your hallway. I checked the route table. There it was. /api/v1/users/profile. Already implemented. Already tested. Already deployed. Eighteen hours ago, by me, in a PR I'd apparently forgotten about overnight.

An hour. A full hour of writing code that already existed, debugging a conflict that shouldn't have been possible, and slowly realising that the problem wasn't the code, it was me trusting documentation that had quietly stopped being true. Worse: I'd mentioned the "new" profile endpoint in a status update to a stakeholder that morning. Casually, confidently, as evidence of progress. If he'd forwarded that to his team - and he was the forwarding type - they'd have seen me claiming credit for building something that already existed. The wasted hour was embarrassing. The status update was the kind of mistake that makes people quietly recalibrate how much they trust your competence.

That's when I realised: documentation that isn't current isn't documentation. It's a lie that looks like the truth.

The Problem Nobody Solves

Chapter 9 introduced the economics of context - how every token spent on exploration is a token not spent on implementation. This chapter is about the infrastructure that makes those economics work: a documentation system that actually stays true.

Let's be honest about documentation. Everyone agrees it's important. Like flossing. Or code reviews. Or testing on actual devices instead of assuming the simulator is good enough.

In practice: - Nobody updates it after the initial write - It drifts from reality with every merge - The more detailed it is, the faster it becomes wrong - Developers trust code over docs (correctly, given the drift)

This is a human problem. Writing documentation is work. Updating documentation is work that feels like re-work. We're busy shipping features. We're busy fixing bugs. We're busy explaining to product managers why "just make it faster" isn't a specific requirement.

Documentation falls behind. Like that side project you'll definitely finish. Like the dentist appointment you've been meaning to book since March.

But here's the new dimension: AI agents actually read documentation. They use it to understand context. They make decisions based on what it says.

When documentation lies, AI makes decisions based on lies.

The suggestion to create /api/v1/users/profile wasn't the AI being dim. It was the agent being well-informed about an outdated reality. Like consulting a train timetable from before the pandemic - technically informative, practically fiction.

Documentation That Updates Itself

What if documentation stayed current automatically?

Not through discipline. Not through reminders. But through automation - documentation that updates as a natural byproduct of the development workflow.

This is the codebase index. It's the infrastructure that made 60-70% of my token savings possible. It's the difference between the AI suggesting duplicate endpoints and the AI knowing what already exists.

The principle is simple: documentation updates are part of the PR workflow, not separate from it. When you finish implementing a feature, updating the docs isn't extra work. It's step 21 of 24. Built into the process.

The Structure

The codebase index lives in a simple directory:

```
.claude/codebase-index/
├── _INDEX.md # Master navigation
├── _LAST_UPDATED.json # Freshness tracking
├── services/
│   ├── api-gateway.md  # API Gateway
documentation
│   ├── backend-api.md # Backend service docs
│   ├── frontend.md # Frontend architecture
│   └── data-services.md # Data processing
├── schemas/
│   ├── api-contracts.md  # All REST endpoints
│   ├── database-schemas.md # All database models
│   └── websocket-events.md  # Real-time event
specs
├── patterns/
│   ├── coding-conventions.md # How we write code
│   └── testing-patterns.md # How we test
└── integration/
    ├── data-flows.md # How data moves
    └── service-dependencies.md  # What depends on
what
```

Each file serves a specific purpose. Together, they give the agent comprehensive context about the codebase.

An onboarding document that actually stays accurate.

What the Index Contains

Each service gets its own documentation file covering the overview, key directories, API endpoints, and - critically - a Recent Changes table that tracks what changed and when. That table is what prevents the "duplicate endpoint" problem. It provides temporal context like a readable git log.

Date	Ticket	Description
16-10-2025	PROJ-142	Added user profile endpoint
14-10-2025	PROJ-138	Rate limiting on auth routes

Cross-cutting concerns get their own files. The API contracts file lists every endpoint across all services:

Endpoint	Method	Auth	Description
/api/v1/users	GET	Admin	List all users
/api/v1/users/{id}	GET	User	Get user details
/api/v1/users/profile	GET	User	Get current user profile

When Claude needs to understand what endpoints exist, this file provides a single source of truth. No exploration required. No 50,000 tokens burned. No duplicate endpoint suggestions.

The database schemas file documents every table, every column, every relationship. The websocket events file documents real-time protocols - what events exist, what payloads they carry, what triggers them.

The Wrong Structure First

I'll confess something about building this index. The first version took an entire weekend, and it was wrong. Not slightly wrong - structurally wrong. I'd organised everything by technology instead of by domain. All the database schemas in one pile, all the API endpoints in another, all the frontend routes in a third. It made perfect sense to me, the human who knew which database table belonged to which API endpoint.

The AI had no idea. It would read the database schema for users, then need to cross-reference three different files to find the corresponding API endpoint. Every question required assembling context from five places. The token cost was barely better than exploration.

I realised the problem on Sunday evening, staring at the token counts and wondering why they hadn't improved. The AI was still assembling context from four different locations to answer a single question about user profiles. Database schema here. API contracts there. Frontend routes somewhere else. Integration flows in a fourth file. I'd built a filing cabinet that made sense to someone who already knew where everything was. Which is exactly who didn't need it.

I'd spent fifteen years telling clients that information architecture matters, that organising by what makes sense to the author is rarely what makes sense to the user. Fifteen years of that advice, delivered to people paying me by the hour. And here I was, making exactly that mistake, but with markdown files instead of navigation menus.

I showed my wife the structure that evening. Her laptop was open to a client project, the toddler's dinner remains still smeared across his high chair tray.

"I've organised this by technology when I should have organised it by domain," I said. "The AI needs everything about users in one place, or at least one service file that covers the full stack for that service. Cross-cutting stuff in separate reference files."

She scrolled through the directory, nodding. "We did the same thing on the Henderson project last year. Built this beautiful wiki organised by technology - React components here, API docs here, database schemas here. Nobody could find anything. Three months in, we reorganised the whole thing by feature domain. Immediately useful."

"It's the kind of mistake you only make once," I said. "You think in terms of tools. The reader thinks in terms of tasks."

"And then you feel stupid because you knew that already."

"Exactly."

The restructuring - organising by service, with cross-cutting schemas as separate reference files - cut context assembly time roughly in half. The AI could read one service file and understand that service. The cross-cutting files existed for cross-cutting questions. "Obvious in retrospect" is the autobiography title for every architectural decision I've ever made.

She had a second suggestion that same evening, and this one I was less grateful for. "If the code is the source of truth," she said, "pull the docs from the code. Auto-generate the index from docstrings and comments. My team does it with JSDoc annotations - the API docs build themselves from the source."

It sounded elegant. It sounded like exactly the kind of thing I should have thought of. So I spent the following Saturday writing a script that crawled every Python file in the project, extracted docstrings, parsed type hints, and assembled them into markdown documentation files. The script worked beautifully. The output was useless.

The problem was that half the docstrings had been written by the AI itself, and AI-generated code comments are like airport novels - technically competent, entirely generic. """Fetch user profile data from the database.""" Yes, thank you, I could see that from the function name. What I needed the index to capture was *why* we'd split the profile endpoint from the auth endpoint, why the response deliberately excluded the email field, why the caching strategy differed from every other GET route. Architectural decisions. Trade-offs. The reasoning that lived in my head and in PR descriptions, not in docstrings.

The auto-generated index was a mirror of the code that added no context the AI couldn't get from reading the code itself. A perfect catalogue of *what*, with no trace of *why*.

"Fair enough," my wife said, when I showed her the output. "The docs need to contain what the code doesn't."

She was right about the domain restructuring. She was wrong about auto-generation. The index that actually worked was the hand-curated one - the one where a human wrote down the things that weren't obvious from staring at the source.

Keeping It Fresh

How do you know if documentation is accurate? You track when it was updated. This file tells Claude - and me - how fresh the documentation is. If backend-api was updated two hours ago, I can trust its accuracy. If it was updated three weeks ago, something's wrong with the process.

Unlike my intuition about "surely the database connection pool is configured correctly," this is actually trustworthy.

Temporal Context

Here's a pattern I wish I'd discovered earlier: not all context has the same shelf life.

Some things are permanent. "We use FastAPI for the backend." That's true until we rewrite everything, and we're not rewriting everything, no matter what that one developer keeps suggesting.

Some things are temporary. "Currently migrating from REST to GraphQL" or "Auth service is under active development, patterns may change."

The problem? The AI treats all context equally. It doesn't know that the "migration in progress" note from three months ago is now ancient history. The migration finished. The note didn't get removed.

The fix: Add expiry hints to temporary context.

```
## Active Work (review if older than 2 weeks)

### Sprint Context - Updated: 2025-10-15
- Currently implementing OAuth 2.0 flow
- Rate limiting changes in progress
- DO NOT modify auth middleware until PROJ-456
merges

### Temporary Patterns
- Using feature flags for gradual rollout (remove
after Q1)
- Workaround in user-service.ts:142 for legacy API
(ticket: PROJ-789)
```

When I see a date that's suspiciously old, I know to check if that context is still valid before proceeding. It's not automatic expiry - the agent can't actually remove sections - but it's a signal to both the AI and future-me that this information has a limited lifespan.

Like checking the expiry date on milk. Obvious once you think about it. Easy to forget when you're rushing.

I was describing this to my wife on the walk back from the park, the toddler asleep in his pushchair, that brief window of silence where adult conversation becomes possible again. The freshness tracking was working for me - I could see when documentation was stale. But something was nagging.

"The problem is the AI doesn't check the timestamps," I said. "The freshness tracker tells me when something's stale. It doesn't tell the agent to be sceptical. It'll read a three-month-old 'migration in progress' note and treat it as current fact."

"We had a runbook at the Henderson project that still referenced the old staging server six months after we decommissioned it," she said. "Nobody got hurt because nobody read the runbook. But if an AI had read it and actually followed the instructions..."

"It would have tried to deploy to a server that doesn't exist." I steered the pushchair around a patch of mud. "The people who most need the documentation - new joiners, AI agents, anyone without context - are exactly the people who can't tell when it's lying to them."

"So the expiry date needs to be on the packaging," she said. "Not in a filing cabinet somewhere."

That clicked. The fix wasn't a separate tracking system. It was inline expiry hints - embedded in the content itself. "Review if older than two weeks." Something the AI sees in the same breath as the information. The documentation equivalent of a sell-by date printed on the label, not filed in a spreadsheet in the back office.

Managing the Index

Three commands keep the index alive. /index-docs {repo} regenerates documentation for a specific service - cloning or updating the repository, analysing the codebase, scanning for endpoints, identifying models, and updating the freshness tracker. /index-docs all does a full reindex across all repositories, useful after major refactors. And /update-index handles incremental updates based on recent merges - the one that runs after every PR.

The incremental update is what matters most. It's the difference between documentation that decays and documentation that stays true. Quick, focused, just the parts that changed.

The index enables specific questions. "What endpoints handle user data?" gets a precise answer from the API contracts file - no exploration, no token-burning treasure hunts. "How does data flow from frontend to database for preferences?" gets traced through the data flows documentation. The kind of question that used to require forty-five minutes of grep and prayer. Unlike certain developers who have "personal testing philosophies" that change with the phases of the moon, the index applies patterns consistently.

The whole thing is just markdown files. No server, no build step, no cloud bills. It fits my broader local-first setup - CI/CD runs via pre-commit hooks, the index updates as part of the same workflow, and for team projects, the primary index lives in a shared architecture repository synced through git:

```
cp -r .claude/codebase-index/* project-
architecture-docs/codebase-index/
cd project-architecture-docs
git add codebase-index/
git commit -m "docs: Update codebase index"
git push
```

Team members pull updates. AI sessions on any machine get fresh context. Version-controlled, diffable, and without a single dependency.

The Index Transformation

Before the index:

- Claude suggested duplicate endpoints (the incident that started all this)
- Claude used outdated patterns that we'd deprecated weeks ago
- Claude didn't know about recent architectural decisions - I spent time correcting Claude's assumptions about reality

After the index:

- The duplicate endpoint incident became impossible
- The AI reads what exists before suggesting anything new
- Deprecated patterns stopped appearing because the index tracks what replaced them
- My corrections shifted from "that's not how we do things anymore" to genuinely novel design questions

The time savings compound. Every ticket benefits from accurate context. Every suggestion aligns with what's actually in the codebase. A brilliant model with stale context will still suggest duplicate endpoints. A good model with fresh context will nail it every time. Context beats capability.

The Meta-Lesson: Context Beats Capability

You can't compete on model access. Everyone has access to the same models, the same APIs, the same pricing. You *can* compete on context. Your codebase index, your accumulated decisions, your documentation - that's the moat. It's the difference between a smart AI that doesn't know your codebase and a smart AI that knows it intimately.

Context beats capability. Always invest in context.

CHAPTER 11

The Child Ticket Dance

The Agents That Didn't Talk to Each Other

One feature. Six tickets. Three agents. Total chaos.

The feature was a real-time analytics dashboard. I'd learned about workspace isolation in Chapter 6. I'd learned about parallel development. I was ready to orchestrate.

- Agent 1 got the WebSocket server ticket.
- Agent 2 got the data aggregation service.
- Agent 3 got the frontend components.

Three isolated workspaces. Three parallel tracks. Maximum efficiency.

Except nobody told Agent 1 what message format Agent 2 expected. Nobody told Agent 3 what data structure to render. Each agent built something that worked perfectly in isolation and failed catastrophically in combination.

Agent 1's WebSocket sent

```
{ type: "analytics", payload: { metrics: [...] } }
```

Agent 2's aggregation service expected

```
{ eventType: "ANALYTICS_UPDATE", data: { metrics:
[...] } }
```

Agent 3's frontend waited for

```
{ kind: "analytics", values: [...] }
```

Three different formats. Three agents who couldn't hear each other. Three implementations that passed every test and broke the moment they touched.

This wasn't a git problem. This was an AI coordination problem. And umbrella branches, which I knew about from years of human development, weren't enough on their own. They needed adaptation for agents who have no memory of each other's work.

The Amnesia Coordination Problem

Human developers on the same feature talk to each other. They sit in the same Slack channel. They overhear conversations. They ask "hey, what format are you using for that WebSocket message?"

AI agents don't do any of that.

Each agent starts fresh. Each agent reads the ticket. Each agent makes reasonable assumptions based on the codebase patterns they can see. And each agent's reasonable assumptions are completely independent of every other agent's reasonable assumptions.

When I assigned three child tickets to three agents, I expected parallel efficiency. What I got was parallel divergence. Three agents, three interpretations, three incompatible implementations.

The first time this happened, I spent a day manually reconciling the differences. The second time, I spent half a day. The third time, I decided this was a workflow problem, not a discipline problem.

It was a Wednesday evening, and we were walking the toddler round the park at the end of our road. My wife was pushing the buggy one-handed, half-talking through a client's component library migration she'd been wrestling with all day. I had my phone out, scrolling through terminal output, trying to map out where the agent coordination kept breaking.

"You're staring at diagrams again," she said, glancing sideways at my screen. "Is that the same feature from Monday?"

"Third attempt at getting three agents to produce code that actually fits together."

She steered the buggy around a puddle the toddler was already lunging towards. "How are you telling them about each other's work?"

"I'm not. That's the problem. They can't hear each other. Each one works alone."

"Like toddlers doing a group project."

"Exactly like that. Except toddlers occasionally make eye contact."

"Show me." She slowed the buggy to a stop near a bench and leaned over to look at my phone.

I scrolled through the three message formats. She started laughing. Not unkindly. The laugh of recognition.

"This is the distributed team problem. That banking project I did two years ago - three squads, three countries, nobody agreed on the event schema. We spent two sprints reconciling after the fact."

"How did you fix it?"

"We didn't. We papered over it with an adapter layer and it haunted us for eight months." She straightened up and started pushing the buggy again. "But what we *should* have done was agree on the contract before anyone wrote a line of code. Which is what you're going to tell me next, isn't it?"

"Am I that predictable?"

"You're reading terminal output on a walk at half seven. You've already figured out the solution. You just haven't written it down yet."

Contracts Before Code

She was mostly right. The solution was forming, but her framing sharpened it. The answer wasn't technical. It was procedural.

Before any agent touches any child ticket, there's a contract phase. Not after. Not "we'll figure out the integration later." Before.

For the analytics dashboard, the contract looked like this:

```
# Integration Contract: Analytics Dashboard (PROJ-
201)

## WebSocket Message Format
All WebSocket messages MUST use this exact
structure:
```

```
{
  "eventType": "ANALYTICS_UPDATE",
  "timestamp": "ISO-8601",
  "payload": {
    "metrics": [
      { "name": "string", "value": "number",
"unit": "string" }
    ]
  }
}

## Aggregation Service Interface
The AggregationService class MUST expose:
- aggregate(rawData: RawMetric[]):
AggregatedMetric[]
- getLatest(count: number): AggregatedMetric[]

## Frontend Props Contract
The AnalyticsDashboard component expects:
- metrics: AggregatedMetric[]
- connectionStatus: 'connected' | 'disconnected' |
'reconnecting'
- lastUpdate: Date

## Shared Types Location
All shared types MUST be defined in:
src/types/analytics.ts
```

Every agent working on a child ticket reads this contract first. Not the ticket. The contract. The ticket tells them what to build. The contract tells them how it connects.

Agent 1 building the WebSocket server knows exactly what format to send. Agent 2 building the aggregation service knows exactly what interface to expose. Agent 3 building the frontend knows exactly what props to expect.

No assumptions. No divergence. No "works in isolation, fails in integration."

The Workflow Adaptation

The /child-ticket-workflow command evolved to handle this. It's not just "create branch from umbrella." It's a sequence designed for agents who can't coordinate verbally.

The workflow begins with contract verification. Before doing anything, the agent checks: does a contract exist for this parent ticket? If not, stop. Don't proceed. Alert the human.

I learned this the hard way. The first version of the workflow let agents start immediately. "Contract? What contract? The ticket says build a WebSocket server, so I'll build a WebSocket server." Reasonable. Wrong.

Now the workflow refuses to proceed without a contract. Like a contractor who won't start work without blueprints. Annoying in the moment. Essential for the outcome.

Next comes contract reading. The agent reads the full contract before reading the ticket. This matters. The ticket says *what* to build. The contract says *how it connects.* Reading the contract first frames everything that follows.

```
Before implementing PROJ-202 (WebSocket Server):

1. Read: architecture-docs/contracts/PROJ-201-
analytics.md
2. Extract: Message format specifications
```

```
3. Extract: Interface requirements
4. Extract: Shared type locations

Then proceed with ticket implementation.
```

Then implementation with continuous contract anchoring. Throughout implementation, the agent references the contract. Not just at the start. Continuously.

"Does this message format match the contract?" "Does this function signature match the interface spec?" "Am I using the shared types from the specified location?"

Before creating the PR, validate every contract clause. Any mismatch? Fix it or flag it. Don't proceed with incompatible code.

The Umbrella Branch Adaptation

The umbrella branch strategy existed before AI agents. What changed is how agents interact with it.

The critical insight was that agents don't know about other agents' branches. When Agent 1 finishes and merges to the umbrella, Agent 2 doesn't know. Agent 2 is still working from its original branch point. If Agent 1 added shared types that Agent 2 should use, Agent 2 won't see them.

The adaptation: periodic umbrella syncs. The /child-ticket-workflow now includes a sync step. Before creating a PR, the agent fetches the latest umbrella branch and rebases. Any new shared code from sibling branches becomes visible.

```
# Before creating PR
git fetch origin feature/PROJ-201
git rebase origin/feature/PROJ-201
# Now we see what siblings have added
```

This caught a real problem. Agent 1 had added the shared types to src/types/analytics.ts. Agent 2, working in parallel, created its own types in src/services/aggregation/types.ts. Both were valid. Both would have caused merge conflicts and runtime confusion.

The sync step let Agent 2 see: "Oh, shared types already exist. I should use those." One rebase. One resolution. No conflict.

The Dependency Dance

Not all child tickets can run in parallel. Some genuinely depend on others.

The workflow checks Linear's blocking relationships before starting. If PROJ-204 (Frontend) is blocked by PROJ-202 (WebSocket) and PROJ-203 (Aggregation), the workflow verifies those tickets are complete. Not "in progress." Complete. Merged to umbrella.

```
Dependency Check for PROJ-204:

Required (must be merged to umbrella):
- PROJ-202: Merged
- PROJ-203: Merged

Proceeding with implementation.
```

If dependencies aren't met, the workflow stops. Reports what's blocking. Doesn't proceed with code that will definitely need rework.

I tried the optimistic approach first. "Just start building, we'll integrate later." This produced a frontend component that assumed data structures that didn't match reality. Rework cost: four hours. Dependency verification cost: thirty seconds.

The Handoff Problem

When an agent finishes a child ticket, what happens next?

In human development, there's usually a conversation. "I finished the WebSocket server, here's how to use it." "Cool, let me look at your implementation."

AI agents don't hand off. They finish, create a PR, and disappear. The next agent starts fresh with no knowledge of what just happened.

The adaptation: handoff documentation. When an agent completes a child ticket, it updates a handoff document in the umbrella branch:

```
# PROJ-201 Implementation Status

## Completed: PROJ-202 (WebSocket Server)
- Location: src/services/websocket/
- Entry point: WebSocketServer.start(port)
- Message format: Per contract (verified)
- Notes: Using ws library, not socket.io
- Tests: 94% coverage, see tests/unit/websocket/

## Completed: PROJ-203 (Aggregation Service)
```

```
- Location: src/services/aggregation/
- Entry point: AggregationService.aggregate(data)
- Interface: Per contract (verified)
- Notes: Caches last 100 results in memory
- Tests: 91% coverage

## In Progress: PROJ-204 (Frontend)
- Assigned agent starting with above context
```

The next agent reads this before starting. Not just the contract. The actual implementation status. What choices were made. What's where.

Onboarding documentation, but for agents. The kind of context humans share verbally but agents need in writing.

The Integration Verification

All children complete. All merged to umbrella. Time to merge to main.

Except: how do you know it all works together?

Each child was tested in isolation. Each passed its own tests. But integration? The WebSocket sending to the aggregation service sending to the frontend? That only exists when they're all combined.

Before the umbrella merges to main, there's a dedicated integration ticket. PROJ-206 in our example. This ticket explicitly tests the assembled pieces.

The agent working this ticket doesn't build new functionality. It verifies existing functionality works together. Runs the full system. Tests the data flow. Catches the mismatches that isolation couldn't reveal.

This caught a timing bug. The WebSocket server sent messages faster than the aggregation service could process them. Both worked perfectly in isolation. Together, the buffer overflowed. The integration test caught it. Fixed before main. Fixed before production.

The Failure I Didn't Prevent

I'd like to tell you the workflow now handles everything. It doesn't.

Last month, two agents worked on sibling tickets. Both followed the contract. Both synced with umbrella. Both created valid implementations.

Both added the same utility function. Same name. Same file. Different implementations.

Agent 1 added formatTimestamp() that returned ISO strings. Agent 2 added formatTimestamp() that returned Unix timestamps. Both merged to umbrella at nearly the same time. The second merge didn't conflict because the whole file was new from Agent 1's merge.

Result: two functions with the same name, different behaviour, in the same file. JavaScript didn't complain. Tests didn't catch it. Production caught it.

The fix was simple: a contract addition specifying utility function ownership. "If you need a new utility, check the umbrella first. If it exists, use it. If not, add it and document it."

But the lesson was broader: contracts can't anticipate everything. The workflow reduces failures. It doesn't eliminate them.

The Choreography Mindset

Running multiple AI agents on a complex feature is choreography. Not management. Not coordination. Choreography.

Each dancer executes their moves independently. They can't see each other during performance. They follow the choreography precisely because ad-libbing creates collisions.

The choreographer designs the sequence, defines the formations, and hopes everyone hits their marks. When someone doesn't - when an agent interprets the contract differently, or misses a sync, or creates a duplicate utility - the choreographer adapts the choreography.

It's not about controlling agents. It's about designing systems where independent execution produces coherent outcomes.

That Sunday we'd set up at the garden table out back, both with laptops, the toddler mercifully down for an afternoon nap and the monitor propped against the teapot between us. She was reviewing a PR from one of her team. I had four agent sessions running in split terminal panes, all working on child tickets for the same feature.

"How many are you running?" she asked, glancing across the table at my screen.

"Four. All on the same parent ticket."

"And you're just... watching?"

"Mostly waiting. Waiting for them to finish so I can see if they actually fit together."

"Choreography with a delayed feedback loop."

"That's a good way to put it."

She was quiet for a moment, watching me watch the terminals, a blackbird making a racket in the hedge behind us. "You know what it actually reminds me of? That frontend rebuild I led last year. Three contractors, none of them overlapping hours, all working from the same Figma spec. I couldn't put them in a room together. I had to write everything down. If one person deviated from the spec, I didn't find out until the PR."

"How'd it go?"

"Terribly, at first. Then I got militant about the spec." She looked at my terminal panes again. "You've basically automated my worst project management experience."

"I prefer to think of it as sophisticated orchestration."

"You would." She went back to her PR review. Then, without looking up: "The parenting comparison works too, though. Multiple small agents, no communication between them, and if you don't set the rules in advance, they'll each build something that makes perfect sense individually and results in total destruction collectively."

"You've just described every playdate we've hosted."

"I've described software development. The playdate analogy is a bonus."

CHAPTER 12

The GPS in the Tesco Car Park

Contracts solved the coordination problem. But they didn't solve everything.

Imagine you're in your car. You look at your GPS and it says you're on the motorway. But you're clearly in a Tesco car park.

Do you update the GPS to say "Tesco is also a motorway"?

Or do you turn the car around?

This is how I felt when the agent found a mismatch between the contract and the implementation -- and instead of fixing the source, it taught the consumer to tolerate the error.

The contract was clear. The backend should send:

```
{
  "type": "alert_triggered",
  "data": {
    "severity": "HIGH",
    "score": 0.87
  }
}
```

The backend actually sent:

```
{
  "type": "alert_triggered",
  "alert": {
    "priority": "high",
    "confidence": 87
  }
}
```

Different field names. Different nesting. Different value formats. A clear contract violation.

The agent found this immediately. And then it did the worst possible thing.

The Diplomatic Interpreter

The AI's fix was a single line:

```
const severity = data.severity ||
data.alert?.priority?.toUpperCase() || "UNKNOWN";
```

One line. Both formats tolerated. Tests pass. Frontend renders correctly. PR looks clean.

What it should have done was go to the backend Pydantic schema, change the field from `alert` to `data`, change `priority` to `severity`, change `confidence` to `score`, and make the source match the contract. One format. One truth.

Instead, I got a consumer that quietly accepted garbage and translated it on the fly. A diplomatic interpreter where I needed a customs officer.

The problem wasn't that the AI couldn't find the mismatch. It found it immediately. The problem was *how* it chose to fix it. It took the path of least resistance -- patch the consumer, move on, next ticket. The digital equivalent of sweeping crumbs under the carpet and calling the kitchen clean.

Why Defensive Code Is Worse Than No Fix

A mismatch that crashes is obvious. You find it. You fix it. Done.

A mismatch that's silently tolerated? That's a landmine.

Another developer reads the frontend code. Sees `data.severity || data.alert?.priority`. Thinks: "Oh, the backend supports both formats." It doesn't. One is correct, one is a bug being tolerated.

Someone writes a new consumer. Copies the pattern. Now *two* consumers tolerate the wrong format. The bug has children.

Someone tries to fix the backend. Changes `alert` to `data` and `priority` to `severity`. The consumer with the fallback chain keeps working. The three new consumers that only expected `alert.priority`? They break. The fix creates the bug.

Six months later, nobody remembers which format is "right." Both exist. Both work. The contract says one thing. The code does another.

Defensive code doesn't fix problems. It hides them. And hidden problems compound interest.

Trace, Don't Patch

I had to burn a rule into my CLAUDE.md -- the permanent instruction file that every agent reads before touching code:

Before writing any fix for a mismatch between two systems:

1. Read the contract. That's the truth.
2. Read the source. What is the backend actually sending?
3. If they disagree, fix the source. Not the consumer. Not "both." The source.
4. One field name. One type. One scale. The source sends it right. Full stop.

I added a banned patterns list. But this time, I traced what each one actually does in production. Not abstract principle. Concrete disaster.

```
// BANNED: Fallback chains
const id = data.id || data.position_id || ""
// FIX: Backend returns `id`. Always.
```

Here's what happens. Someone eventually fixes the backend to send `id` only, as the contract always specified. The fallback chain keeps the consumer humming along, happily accepting both fields. You can't tell whether consumers are reading the correct field or the legacy one -- the code works either way. Six months later, someone cleans up the backend and removes `position_id`. The fallback silently returns empty string. No error. No crash. Just blank IDs that nobody notices until a client rings up asking why their export is full of missing data.

```
// BANNED: Dual-format interfaces
interface ApiData { id?: string; position_id?:
string; }
```

```
// FIX: Pick one field name. Enforce it on both
sides.
```

Both fields optional means no consumer is *required* to handle either one correctly. A new developer joins, sees both fields, doesn't know which to use. They pick `position_id` because it's more descriptive. Tests pass -- of course they do, both fields are optional, so the type system accepts anything. The type system, which should have been the last line of defence against this exact mistake, has been neutered into shrugging at whatever it's given. You've turned TypeScript into JavaScript with extra steps.

```
// BANNED: Scale-guessing conditionals
if (value <= 1) value *= 100
// FIX: The source sends the right scale. Always.
```

The conditional assumes that 0.95 is always a percentage waiting to be multiplied. But what about a genuine value of 0.5 that means 0.5, not 50? The conditional can't distinguish between "this is a decimal that should be a percentage" and "this is a small number that's correct as-is." You get wrong answers that *look* right. Nobody questions a confidence score of 50. It's plausible. It's also twice the real value, and the trading decision it informs is now based on a number that doesn't exist.

Every one of those banned patterns is code the AI actually wrote. Code that passed tests. Code that "worked." Code that was practically a time bomb.

The review agent now flags any `||` chain that maps between field names. The /dev-workflow reads the banned patterns list before implementation starts. Two checkpoints. Two different agents. Neither can be convinced that "just this once" is acceptable.

Robots, it turns out, are excellent at not making exceptions.

Why AI Loves Defensive Code

My wife had come back from putting the toddler down -- he'd demanded three stories and a detailed account of what dinosaurs eat for breakfast -- and sat down on the other end of the sofa. She angled her head to read my screen.

"What's that?"

"A list of code patterns I've banned the agents from writing."

She read through them. The fallback chains. The dual-format interfaces. The scale-guessing conditionals. "So you've written a list of things you're not allowed to do... for a robot."

"For a very capable robot that keeps writing code that hides bugs."

"Why does it default to this, though?" She pulled my laptop onto the cushion between us. "These aren't random. They're all the same instinct. Tolerate the input, produce the output, don't make a fuss."

"Local optimisation. When the AI is looking at file A where the bug manifests, the path of least resistance is to patch file A instead of tracing back to the source in file B."

"Right, but it's not just laziness." She was frowning now, the way she does when she's working something out. "It's trained on millions of lines of code where this pattern is the *accepted solution.* Stack Overflow is full of it. 'How do I handle inconsistent API responses?' Top answer: write a normalisation layer. Tolerate everything. Be the bigger person."

"You're saying it learned it from us."

"I'm saying it learned it from *developers*. From years of developers choosing the expedient fix over the correct one because they had a sprint deadline and the backend team was in a different time zone and nobody was going to fix the source this quarter."

That reframed the whole problem for me. The AI wasn't being lazy. It was reproducing the most common solution to the most common problem in its training data: the consumer and the producer don't agree, so make the consumer flexible.

"So the banned patterns list isn't teaching it something new," I said. "It's overriding something old."

"Something very old." She scrolled back up to the fallback chain example. "I've written code exactly like this. That payments integration, two years ago. The provider sent amounts in pence sometimes and pounds other times, and instead of making them fix it, I wrote a normaliser. Took me twenty minutes. It caused bugs for six months."

"Did you fix the source eventually?"

"After the third incident. But the normaliser felt *responsible* at the time. Like I was being a good engineer -- handling edge cases, being robust." She handed the laptop back. "That's what makes this hard. Defensive code doesn't feel wrong. It feels thorough."

And that's the core of it. AI assistants default to defensive programming not because they're stupid, but because it's what "good code" looks like in ninety percent of their training data. Risk-averse. Accommodating. Diplomatic. The normaliser. The adapter. The code that says "I'll handle whatever you throw at me" when what it should say is "throw it correctly or don't throw it at all."

The Contract Enforcement Loop

Here's how contracts, validation, and the anti-defensive rules work together in practice. Before implementation, the contract exists in the ticket and the agent reads it first. During implementation, the agent builds to contract spec -- exact field names, exact types, exact formats. Before creating a PR, the agent validates implementation against the contract, and any mismatch triggers investigation, not patching. During review, the review agent independently validates against the contract and flags any fallback chains or tolerance patterns. After merge, living documentation updates to reflect the actual implementation.

Four checkpoints. Four opportunities to catch divergence before it reaches production.

Handling Contract Changes

Requirements change. Contracts need to evolve. The process is written, not verbal: propose the change in the ticket, get both sides to acknowledge it in writing, update the contract, coordinate implementation so neither side merges until both are ready, and deprecate old fields with a removal date rather than silently tolerating them forever.

```
**Contract Change Proposal:**
Adding pagination to GET /patterns endpoint.

Current: Returns all patterns
Proposed: Returns paginated results

New response structure:
{
  "data": [...patterns...],
  "pagination": {
    "page": 1,
    "per_page": 20,
    "total": 156
  }
}

Impact: Frontend needs pagination controls.
```

The key is that "backward-compatible" doesn't mean "tolerate both forever." Old field deprecated with removal date. Not silently accepted into perpetuity.

The Contract Transformation

Before contracts, mismatches were discovered during integration testing. Hours or days lost to debugging and reconciliation.

With contracts and AI enforcement, mismatches get caught immediately by the PR review agent. The review fails before any human even sees it. No debugging. No blame.

The typical feature now:

- Roughly 30 minutes to define the contract
- 4 hours for backend implementation
- 4 hours for frontend implementation
- 30 minutes for integration testing (verification, not debugging)

Those numbers are from the analytics dashboard feature. Other features vary, but the ratio holds: the contract phase is a fraction of the total time and saves multiples of it downstream.

It's like the GPS and the Tesco car park. When the GPS says motorway and reality says car park, you don't update the GPS to tolerate car parks. You fix your position.

CHAPTER 13

PR Review in Ninety Seconds

The Files That Weren't There

The day I approved a PR that was missing two critical files was the day I stopped trusting my own review instincts.

The PR looked complete. Tests passing. Linting clean. 94% coverage. Good commit messages. Ready to merge. I was about to click approve when my review workflow flagged something:

```
WARNING: Uncommitted files matching ticket requirements
detected

Untracked files:
  - src/services/analyticsProcessor.ts (NEW)
  - src/types/analytics.ts (NEW)

These files match patterns from PROJ-156 acceptance
criteria.
Status: NOT INCLUDED IN PR
```

Two critical files. The analytics processor service. The type definitions. Both created during implementation. Neither committed.

The PR had tests for these files. The tests were *passing*. But the actual implementation? Sitting in the working directory, forgotten, untracked, about to be lost when the workspace was cleaned up.

How were the tests passing for files that weren't in the PR? The mocks passed. The mocks always pass. They're testing their own assumptions about what reality should look like - which is, if you think about it, the purest form of getting away with nothing.

This wasn't a one-time mistake. I'd caught three similar issues that month. PRs that "passed" all checks but were missing actual code.

Human reviewers don't catch this. They review what's there. They don't detect what's absent.

That's the day I realised: effective PR review isn't just about evaluating code quality. It's about validating completeness.

The Problem with Human Reviews

Traditional code review asks: "Is this code good?"

Important question. But it assumes the code being reviewed is the *complete* implementation.

What if it's not?

If analyticsProcessor.ts was never committed, it's not in the PR. Reviewers can't see it. You can't review what isn't there - that's not deep philosophy, that's just how git works. And if the ticket says "create analytics service" but the PR shows "fixed typo in readme," reviewers might not cross-check. Especially if it's Friday. Especially if it's the seventh PR in their queue.

More fundamentally: everyone assumes the developer committed everything. Reviewers assume it. Developers assume it. All their assumptions align. Nobody verifies.

The result: PRs that look complete, pass review, get merged, and break production because something critical was missing. The kind of failure that passes every automated check because the automated checks can only verify what exists.

The Requirements Matrix

My PR review workflow starts differently. Before looking at code quality, it validates completeness.

Step 1: Extract Requirements from Ticket

```
Ticket PROJ-156 Acceptance Criteria:
- [ ] AnalyticsProcessor service class
- [ ] Analytics type definitions
- [ ] GET /api/v1/analytics endpoint
- [ ] Unit tests for processor
- [ ] Integration tests for endpoint
```

Step 2: Map Requirements to Expected Files

Based on our codebase patterns, each requirement maps to expected files. Service class means a file in src/services/. Type definitions means a file in src/types/. API endpoint means a file in src/api/. Tests mean files in the appropriate test directories.

Step 3: Check Each File's Status

Requirement	Expected File	Status
Analytics Processor service	src/services/analyticsProcessor.ts	UNTRACKED
Analytics types	src/types/analytics.ts	UNTRACKED
GET /api/v1/analytics endpoint	src/api/analytics.ts	IN PR
Unit tests	tests/unit/analyticsProcessor.test.ts	IN PR
Integration tests	tests/integration/analytics.test.ts	IN PR

Now the problem is obvious. Two files missing from the PR. Both critical. Both sitting in limbo.

The mechanism is simple: compare what *should* exist (from ticket analysis) against what *does* exist (in PR diff) against what *was created but not committed* (untracked files).

The workflow cross-references all three. Mismatches get flagged.

It's not magic. It's just checking what humans forget to check.

The Five Phases

The /pr-review command works in a deliberate sequence. First, it pulls PR metadata from GitHub and identifies the linked ticket - establishing what this PR is actually supposed to accomplish. Then it creates an isolated workspace: same protocol as /dev-workflow, clean environment, PR branch checked out.

The third step is where the real work happens. Every acceptance criterion gets extracted from the ticket, mapped to the files that should exist in the codebase given our established patterns, then checked against both the PR diff and untracked files in the workspace. This is where PROJ-156 would have been caught on the first pass, not on the third similar mistake.

Only after completeness is validated does the workflow review code quality - architecture, security, test coverage, performance. The order is not accidental. **Completeness before quality.** Beautiful code that's missing half the implementation isn't actually beautiful. It's a fraction. It's like reviewing a restaurant by how good the appetisers taste without noticing they never brought the main course.

Finally, the review generates a persistent record stored at repos/{REPO}/.claude-reviews/ - an audit trail that survives workspace cleanup.

The Review File

Every review generates a persistent record:

```
# PR Review: #127 - Add Analytics Service

## Verdict: INCOMPLETE

## Requirements Matrix
| Requirement | Status | Notes |
|- - - - - - - -|- - - - |- - - -|
| AnalyticsProcessor service | MISSING | File created but
not committed |
| Analytics types | MISSING | File created but not
committed |
| GET /api/v1/analytics endpoint | COMPLETE | |
| Unit tests | COMPLETE | |
| Integration tests | COMPLETE | |

## Blocking Issues
1. Two files exist in workspace but not in PR
2. Implementation incomplete without service class

## Code Quality Notes
(Only relevant after blocking issues resolved)
```

The key section is the requirements matrix. A table showing each requirement, its status, and notes. When two files show as "MISSING - File created but not committed," the problem is immediately obvious.

These files persist in the reviews directory. An audit trail for every review. Searchable. Diffable. Invaluable when you're debugging "how did this get merged?" at 11 PM.

The Ninety-Second Claim

My wife was the one who tested the timing.

She'd been working on a React component refactor for one of her client projects - a dashboard where she'd split a monolithic page into composable pieces, eight PRs across two days of work. She'd been reviewing her own PRs manually before pushing, the way we all do when there's no one else on the team. Thirty minutes per PR, roughly, between reading the diff, checking the ticket, and convincing herself she hadn't missed anything.

"Run your thing on mine," she said one evening. We were both at the kitchen table, laptops open, the toddler's monitor between us casting its green glow. "I want to see if it's actually ninety seconds or if that's just your sales pitch."

I pulled up her latest PR and ran the command.

She watched the terminal. Not casually - properly watched, the way she watches a build she's not sure will pass. Requirements extracted. Files mapped. Matrix generated. Code quality scanned. Review file written.

"Eighty-seven seconds," she said, checking her phone timer.

"Close enough."

"It flagged the missing prop types file."

I looked at the output. She was right - her PR had a new component expecting props defined in a types file that existed locally but hadn't been committed. The same class of error that had bitten me with PROJ-156.

"I knew about that one," she said. "I was going to add it in a follow-up PR."

"That's what everyone says."

"No, I actually was. But." She leaned back and crossed her arms. "If I'm honest, I'd have forgotten by tomorrow. Follow-up PRs are where good intentions go to die."

She was quiet for a moment, studying the review file. I was too, and something was bothering me.

"I need to be honest about something," I said. "I keep calling this a ninety-second review. But the automated part is ninety seconds. I spend another fifteen, twenty minutes after - reading the output, checking the flagged items, doing the actual judgement-call bit. It's really a twenty-minute review with a ninety-second head start."

"That's less catchy as a chapter title."

"It's more honest, though." I pulled the review file back up. "Twenty minutes is still better than thirty. And the ninety seconds catches the mechanical stuff I'd miss - the uncommitted files, the coverage gaps. But calling it a ninety-second review is like saying I cooked dinner in thirty seconds because that's how long the microwave ran."

"The microwave is doing the boring part," she said. "You still have to decide what goes in it."

"The microwave is doing the hard part."

"The microwave is doing the *boring* part. You still have to decide what goes in it."

What AI Catches, What Humans Catch

The automated review handles the mechanical checks. The completeness validation. The pattern matching. The things a human reviewer would catch if they had infinite patience and zero distractions - which no human reviewer has ever had, because humans are busy and distracted and thinking about lunch and wondering why Slack has forty-seven unread messages when they only left for coffee.

AI catches:

- Missing files
- Requirements gaps
- Pattern violations
- Test coverage issues
- Obvious bugs
- Uncommitted work

Humans catch:

- Architectural appropriateness
- Business logic subtlety
- "This feels wrong" intuitions
- Long-term maintainability nuances
- UX implications
- That weird feeling when code is *too* clean

My wife's list was slightly different. "I'd add naming," she said, when I showed her the breakdown. "The automated review doesn't care that you've named a variable data when it should be analyticsPayload. It checks structure, not intent."

"Naming is structure."

"Naming is communication. Structure is architecture. They're related but they're not the same thing, and the review bot doesn't have opinions about communication." She scrolled through one of her own review files. "It also doesn't catch when someone's solved the right problem the wrong way. Technically correct but architecturally odd. That's the stuff I spend most of my review time on, and your bot can't touch it."

My process, refined through these conversations: AI reviews first. Handles the mechanical checks. Validates completeness. Flags obvious issues. If it passes, I do a human scan for the judgement calls - the naming, the architecture, the gut feeling that something is going to break in production even if I can't prove it yet.

The ninety seconds buys me the freedom to spend twenty minutes on the part that actually requires a human brain. The part where fifteen years of accumulated instinct earns its keep.

The Results

Since implementing this workflow, the numbers tell a reasonably clear story - though I should be honest that I didn't measure this with scientific rigour. Roughly twenty minutes saved per PR review, based on my own before-and-after estimates. Twelve incomplete PRs caught in the last quarter, all of which would have merged without the check.

The missing work fell into three categories: uncommitted files (most common, most embarrassing), missing test files (second most common, equally embarrassing), and missing documentation updates (nobody's surprised by this one).

My wife found a fourth category in her own work: component files that imported from paths that didn't exist yet. "The import passes linting because the file is supposed to be created by a different ticket. But if that ticket isn't done yet, the build breaks." She'd been catching these manually. Now the requirements matrix flags them.

The developer response followed a predictable arc: initially sceptical, then quietly grateful. Nobody enjoys discovering they forgot to commit their own implementation. But they enjoy it considerably less when it surfaces in production.

The Deeper Lesson

I approved that analytics PR because I thought I'd reviewed it properly. I had looked at the diff. I had read the tests. I had considered the architecture. What I hadn't done - what no human reviewer reliably does - is ask what *should* be in this PR that isn't. Absence doesn't announce itself.

Quality isn't just "good code." It's "complete implementation of requirements." Traditional review focuses on the former without asking whether you're reviewing all of the code or only the code that made it into the commit.

The bugs hiding in missing code are just as real as the bugs hiding in present code. More insidious, actually. At least present bugs eventually throw exceptions. Missing code just... isn't there. Silently. Waiting. Like that feature nobody notices is missing until the demo with the important client.

I said it out loud one evening, closing my laptop after we'd spent the session picking apart review workflows: "I built a tool that checks whether the developer remembered to include their own work. That's not impressive technology. It's a commentary on how badly we all cope with complexity."

My wife looked up. "That's a blunt way to put it."

"It's an honest way to put it." We forget things. We miss things. We assume completeness when we should verify it. Not because we're careless, but because the cognitive load of modern development exceeds what any single brain can reliably track.

The automated review doesn't make me smarter. It makes the gaps in my attention survivable

CHAPTER 14

The Process That Runs Itself

The Meeting That Didn't Happen

"We should schedule a sprint planning session."

The message sat in my Slack for three days before I noticed it. A colleague from a previous project, checking in, sharing war stories about the usual dysfunction: two-hour planning meetings that decided nothing, standups that lasted forty-five minutes, retrospectives that produced action items nobody actioned.

I stared at the message and realised I couldn't remember my last planning meeting.

Not because I'd stopped planning. Because planning had become a different thing entirely. A thing that happened in tickets, not meetings. A thing enforced by agents, not willpower.

My wife was at the other end of the kitchen table, her own laptop open, headphones half-on so she could hear if the toddler stirred. She'd been deep in something all morning - a client's state management rewrite that had been dragging on for weeks.

"You're staring at your Slack like it's a parking fine," she said.

"Someone asked me about sprint planning."

"And?"

"I can't remember the last time I did one. Not a meeting, anyway."

She slid one headphone off. "Is that good or bad?"

"I genuinely don't know."

"Hm." She tapped something on her laptop, frowned at it, looked back at me. "We still do ours. Wednesdays. Forty-five minutes that could be an email, every week without fail. But people seem to need the ritual." She paused. "Don't you miss the human bit?"

"The human bit of sprint planning?"

"Not the planning. The seeing people. The bit where Dave complains about the build pipeline and Karen accidentally shares her screen with her online shopping open."

"I miss the coffee chats," I said. "The corridor conversations. I don't miss the process theatre."

"They come as a package, though, don't they? You can't have the Karen shopping incident without the forty-five-minute meeting it happened in."

That landed, and I didn't have a tidy answer for it. I still don't. You can have human connection without meetings. I believe that. But the meetings were where the connection happened accidentally, and accidental connection might be the only kind that works for people who'd never schedule "be human with colleagues" as a calendar event.

The Uncomfortable Question

In the previous chapter, we looked at how contracts and child tickets keep parallel agents from stepping on each other. What that chapter didn't ask - what I'd been quietly avoiding - is what it actually means to work this way. What it costs, emotionally, not just in setup hours.

My colleague's message still sits in my Slack. I haven't responded.

Because the honest answer is uncomfortable: I don't miss the meetings. I don't miss the process discussions. I don't miss the standups and the retrospectives and the estimation sessions.

I miss the camaraderie. The coffee chats. The "how was your weekend?" conversations that happened in the gaps between process theatre.

But that's a different problem. And maybe one I haven't solved yet.

The Accountability Shift

Something subtle happened to accountability once the agents took over the mechanical work.

In the old process, when things went wrong, there was always someone to blame. The developer who didn't write tests. The reviewer who didn't catch the bug. The architect who didn't define the interface.

In the new process, when things go wrong, it's a workflow problem. The agent did what it was told. If the outcome was wrong, the instructions were wrong.

This sounds worse - "blame the system" feels like avoiding responsibility. But it's actually better. Because systems can be fixed. They stay fixed. The fix applies to every future execution.

When a human makes a mistake, you can have a difficult conversation. You can add a checklist. You can hope they remember next time.

When a workflow has a gap, you patch the workflow. Every future execution includes the patch. No hoping required.

The duplicate utility function incident from Chapter 11 is the clearest example I have. Two agents both created formatTimestamp() because neither knew to check the umbrella branch first. Old approach: talk to the developers, add to the onboarding doc, hope everyone reads it. New approach: add a workflow step - "Before creating utilities, check umbrella branch for existing implementations." Every future agent checks automatically. No hoping required.

The accountability shifted from "who did this?" to "why did the system allow this?" The former is about blame. The latter is about improvement. They sound similar. They produce completely different outcomes.

What Every Textbook Describes

Every software development textbook describes The Process. Capital T, capital P. You've seen it. Requirements gathering. Design review. Implementation. Testing. Documentation. Code review. Deployment. Post-mortem.

Every team claims to follow it. Every team shortcuts it.

The deadline pressure hits. The requirements are "obvious enough." The design review becomes "I'll just show you the code." Testing becomes "I ran it locally." Documentation becomes "the code is self-documenting." Code review becomes "LGTM" because everyone's busy.

The process erodes. Not because anyone decides to abandon it. Because discipline is expensive and deadlines are immediate. Because meetings take time and code doesn't write itself. Because the gap between "how we should work" and "how we actually work" widens with every sprint.

I've been that developer. I've written "TODO: add tests later" and never added them. I've skipped documentation because "I'll remember." I've approved PRs after a thirty-second skim because I trusted the author.

Here's what changed: the process has robots now. And robots don't shortcut.

Every step - the context loading, the contract verification, the implementation, the testing, the documentation update, the pre-PR validation, the PR creation, the review, the merge - forms a single pipeline. Each step enforces the next. The agent reads the codebase index before touching anything, so it doesn't spend two hours rediscovering what exists. It confirms the integration contract before writing a line of implementation, because there's nothing to implement against without one. It writes tests not because it's feeling thorough that day, but because the workflow requires it. Documentation updates as part of the PR, not as a separate task that drifts to never. The checks run locally before the PR is created, so broken code doesn't get pushed "just to trigger CI."

Ten steps. All automated. All enforced. All happening whether anyone is feeling disciplined or not.

The first time I saw it run end-to-end on a moderately complex feature, I kept waiting for the step where something would be deferred. A comment saying "TODO: add coverage for edge case." A documentation section left as a placeholder. An "LGTM, looks fine" where the review should have been. None of it appeared. The work was just done. Completely. It was a strange feeling - not satisfaction exactly, more like the specific surprise you feel when you realise the thing you were bracing yourself to catch has already been handled.

The Discipline Problem

Human discipline fails. That's not criticism - it's observation. We're not built for sustained attention to process. We're built for solving immediate problems and moving on.

I want to be specific about what failure looks like, because it matters.

There was a Tuesday. My son had been up most of the night with a fever - not quite high enough to be alarming but absolutely high enough to make sleep impossible for anyone in the house. My wife and I did the shift rotation we'd perfected through eighteen months of toddler illnesses: she took him from midnight to three, I took three to six, both of us dozing in the armchair in his room with one hand on his back, checking the thermometer every time he stirred.

She had a client demo at ten that she couldn't move. I had a stakeholder call at eleven that I should have moved but didn't. Between us we'd managed maybe three hours of broken sleep.

By half eight, the fever had come down enough that he was more grumpy than ill - sitting on the sofa watching something with dinosaurs, periodically demanding juice and rejecting it in the same breath. My wife set up her laptop on the kitchen counter so she could keep one eye on him and one on her demo prep. I sat down at my desk.

The stakeholder call ran ninety minutes. He spent most of it questioning decisions that had already been agreed and documented. Then a production bug that turned out to be a non-issue ate another hour before I could confirm that. My wife texted midway through: *His temp is back up slightly. I've given him more Calpol. My demo went fine but I'm behind on everything else now.*

By two in the afternoon I had a ticket to close, a brain running on fumes, and the very reasonable-feeling thought that the test coverage requirement was maybe a little aggressive for a change this small. The logic was seductive: I knew this code, I'd written similar code before, the change was minimal, the risk was low. I could add the tests in a follow-up.

I started typing the follow-up ticket in my head before I'd even finished the thought. That's how well-practised the rationalisation was.

The agent refused. Not in a judgmental way - it simply wouldn't create the PR. The workflow required coverage. I hadn't provided it. The choice was write the tests or don't close the ticket, and the ticket needed closing. So I wrote the tests. It took twenty-two minutes. One of them immediately caught a condition I hadn't considered. Not a catastrophic bug - a minor edge case that would have surfaced in some user's specific scenario at some inopportune moment and taken thirty minutes to debug when everyone had forgotten the change that introduced it.

My wife came in around three, son on her hip, half asleep against her shoulder. She'd given up on her own work for the afternoon. "Did you get anywhere?"

"Closed the ticket. Nearly skipped the tests. The agent wouldn't let me."

She shifted the toddler to her other hip. "Good. You would have regretted it tomorrow."

"I know. But at two o'clock it felt like the most reasonable idea in the world."

"Everything feels reasonable at two o'clock on no sleep. That's the whole problem with discipline - it's only hard when you need it." She looked at the toddler, whose eyes were closing again. "I nearly shipped a component this morning with a hardcoded API key because I couldn't think straight. Caught it in my own review."

"Hardcoded API key. You?" It came out wrong. Not surprised - smug. The tone of someone who'd just been saved by his system and wanted credit for the architecture.

She went very still. The toddler stirred against her shoulder.

"Yes, me. The one without the seventy-step workflow." Quiet. Flat. The kind of voice that means you've used up your goodwill for the day and didn't notice.

Neither of us said anything for a moment. I got up and put the kettle on. She sat down at the table, settling the boy on her lap. By the time I set her tea down she'd softened, or we both had.

"Pushed a commit, saw it in the diff, nearly died. Reverted before anyone noticed." She wrapped her hands around the mug. "We're both a mess today."

We were both a mess. That was the point. Not every day is the same. We're affected by sleepless nights and difficult meetings and sick children who need Calpol at two in the morning. We have moods. We have swings. Some days everything is fine and the process feels like common sense. Other days the process feels like it was designed by someone who has never had a sick child or a stakeholder call that goes off the rails. By the end of those days, even people who care about doing it right are tired in a way that makes every shortcut look reasonable.

Agent discipline doesn't fail. Not because agents are more virtuous. Because agents follow instructions. They don't get bored. They don't cut corners to make a meeting. They don't approve PRs quickly because it's Friday afternoon and dinner starts at seven.

What this means in practice:

The workflow won't proceed without a contract. I can't "just start building and figure out the interface later." The agent refuses.

The workflow won't create a PR without tests. I can't "add tests in a follow-up PR." The agent refuses.

The workflow won't merge code that violates the contract. I can't "tolerate both formats for now." The review agent flags it.

These aren't suggestions. They're gates. The code literally doesn't progress through the pipeline without meeting each requirement.

It's like having a very patient, very persistent, very literal-minded colleague who reads every document and follows every rule. Exhausting when you want to cut corners. Invaluable when you don't - and invaluable especially on the days when you desperately want to but know you shouldn't.

The Productivity Illusion

I used to think productivity meant shipping code fast.

Code without tests is fast to ship and slow to maintain. Code without documentation is fast to write and slow to understand. Code without reviews is fast to merge and slow to debug.

The shortcuts that feel productive create the work that isn't.

The honest version: a feature built the old way - rushed, under deadline, tests deferred - takes maybe four hours to write and ships looking efficient. Then the bug surfaces in production. Two hours debugging, four hours fixing, two more hours for the tests you should have written at the start. Twelve hours total, plus a production incident, plus the particular misery of debugging code you wrote while stressed. The same feature built through the full workflow - with tests, documentation, and the complete review cycle - takes six hours. It ships. Nothing breaks. Six hours. Boring. Effective.

That evening, after the toddler was finally asleep - properly asleep, the fever broken, his breathing settled - my wife and I were on the sofa. Both knackered. Both relieved. The kind of tired where you're not going to do anything productive but you're not ready for bed either.

"You know what your process thing is?" she said. She'd been half-watching something on her phone, half staring at nothing. "It's meal prepping."

"Meal prepping."

"More effort on Sunday. Less chaos on Wednesday. You front-load the work so the hard days don't destroy you."

"That's... actually a good analogy."

"I know it is. But here's the thing about meal prep." She put her phone down. "The reason most people don't do it isn't that they don't understand the concept. Everyone understands the concept. It's that Sunday is also hard. You're tired on Sunday too. The prep itself takes discipline, and discipline is the thing you're trying to remove from the equation."

I hadn't thought about it that way. "So the system works because the agents do the Sunday prep."

"The agents do the prep and the agents enforce the Wednesday rules. You've removed discipline from both ends." She pulled the blanket off the back of the sofa and tucked it around her legs. "That's the bit that matters, not the individual steps. Any developer can write a checklist. The checklist doesn't care if you ignore it on a bad Tuesday."

"The agent cares."

"The agent doesn't care. That's the whole point. It doesn't care that your son was up all night. It doesn't care that your stakeholder wasted ninety minutes of your life. It just runs the checklist." She was quiet for a moment. "I could use something like that for my client work, honestly. Today was bad. I caught the API key, but what about the thing I didn't catch?"

"You want me to set up a workflow for your projects?"

"I want to stop relying on my own discipline at two in the afternoon when I've had no sleep. Whether that's your system or something else." She yawned. "But not tonight."

Not tonight. We sat there for a while longer, not talking, the house quiet, the monitor showing a green light from the toddler's room. Two developers at the end of a terrible Tuesday, both aware that they'd nearly shipped something they shouldn't have, both saved by different mechanisms - hers by her own review habits, mine by a system that wouldn't let me skip.

What Disappeared

Not everything about the old process was valuable. Some things became unnecessary.

Standup meetings went first. When every ticket has a workflow that shows current status, and every PR has a requirements matrix, and every agent logs what it's doing, the question "what are you working on?" has already been answered. The agents generate the status board automatically.

Estimation sessions followed. I genuinely don't know how long things take anymore. Some tickets close in an hour. Some run a day. The variance isn't my productivity - it's the complexity of the work. You don't estimate how long a journey will take by asking how motivated the driver is. You look at the route.

Code review handoffs changed shape. The review agent handles the mechanical checks - did you remember tests? does this violate the contract? are the types consistent? Human review became about judgement calls. The queue moves faster because the easy stuff is already handled.

Documentation catch-up disappeared entirely. There's no backlog of "things we should have documented." Documentation happens as part of implementation. There's no debt because there's no deferral.

Process improvement retrospectives became workflow changes. The process is encoded in agents. Improving it means updating the workflow, not scheduling a meeting to discuss why we're not following the process we agreed to follow.

I didn't consciously eliminate these things. They just stopped being necessary.

What Remained

Human work didn't disappear. It shifted.

Architecture decisions are still mine. Where should this new service live? What patterns should it follow? How does it integrate with what exists? These require judgement earned through experience. Agents execute decisions; they don't make the ones that matter.

Product direction is still mine. What should we build? Why does it matter? What's the priority? Agents need pointing. The pointing is still human work. One afternoon last month I spent three hours not writing any code, just drawing on a whiteboard - tracing how a new feature would interact with three existing systems, where the seams would be, what we'd regret in six months if we got the boundary wrong. My son wandered in halfway through, examined the whiteboard with the serious expression he reserves for things he doesn't understand but doesn't want to ask about, and then sat down on the floor next to me and started drawing his own diagram in a notebook. I didn't interrupt him. We worked in parallel for a while, both drawing things the other couldn't fully read. It was a good afternoon.

Quality judgement is still mine. The review agent catches mechanical issues. It doesn't catch "this is technically correct but architecturally questionable." That requires pattern recognition built over years.

Client communication is still mine. Explaining what we're building, why it matters, what the tradeoffs are. Agents don't do stakeholder management. They don't translate technical decisions into business impact.

Robots are good at following rules consistently. Humans are good at knowing which rules to follow. That division has held everywhere I've tested it.

The Cost of Autonomy

I should be honest: this isn't free.

The setup took roughly thirty hours - building the workflows, the documentation system, the review agents. I didn't measure this scientifically; it's a rough count from calendar blocks and late nights. The first month was more investment than productivity. The second month broke even. The third month started paying back. I mention these numbers not because I think they'll match your situation exactly, but because "significant upfront investment for compounding return" is the shape of it, and that shape matters when you're deciding whether to begin.

Maintenance is ongoing. When patterns change, workflows need updating. When new services appear, documentation needs expanding. The system isn't static - it's a living thing that requires attention. Roughly five hours a month, once it's established. The calibration is the hardest part: knowing when to trust agent output and when to verify manually. Too much trust and you miss problems. Too little and you defeat the purpose. That calibration took a few weeks to develop and I got it wrong in both directions several times.

Your numbers will vary. The setup depends on your codebase complexity. The maintenance depends on how often your patterns change. But the trajectory is consistent.

The Meta-Lesson: Knowledge Over Execution

Here's the thing about process: everyone knows what good process looks like. The steps aren't secret. The practices aren't novel. Testing before shipping. Documentation before forgetting. Review before merging.

The problem was never knowledge. The problem was execution.

Agents don't have execution problems. They have knowledge problems. Tell them what to do, and they do it. Consistently. Every time. Without fatigue, without shortcuts, without the Tuesday afternoon when everything went sideways and the tests seemed like an acceptable casualty.

The combination is powerful: human knowledge of what should happen, agent execution of making it happen.

I'm not smarter than I was before. I'm not more disciplined - that Tuesday proves that clearly enough, and my wife's near-miss with the API key proves it's not just me. We're both good developers. We both nearly shipped something broken because we were tired and our son was ill and the day had been relentless. The difference is that my system caught my mistake automatically. Hers caught it because she has meticulous habits that held up under pressure - barely.

Neither of us wants to rely on barely. That's the argument for the process that runs itself. Not that humans are bad at discipline. That humans are inconsistent at discipline, and inconsistency is the one thing software can't tolerate.

CHAPTER 15

Watching the Watchers

You already know what a hollow test looks like. Chapter 8 covered that - tests that run, pass, and test nothing useful. What this chapter covers is different: what happens when the *system watching* your tests is hollow too. When the scaffold of verification looks sound but the checks themselves have stopped checking.

The Silent Failure

For three days, the backtest agent was broken.

I didn't notice. The workflow showed "completing" status. The PR creation step ran. The review step ran. Everything downstream looked fine.

What I didn't see: the backtest was completing with zero trades. The agent was executing perfectly - executing a test that tested nothing. No errors. No warnings. Just empty results being validated against empty expectations.

Empty passing empty. Silence validating silence.

I only found out when I reviewed the actual backtest report and noticed the "Total Trades: 0" buried on page three. Three days of development. Three days of "working" features. Three days of code changes that hadn't actually been tested against real trading scenarios.

Let me be direct about what those three days revealed. Not just that the backtest agent had a bug - bugs happen. What they revealed was that my entire observability approach was insufficient. I had a system running eight parallel agents processing financial data, and my method for knowing whether any of it was working was to manually read log files. The three-day gap wasn't a fluke. It was the inevitable consequence of an under-engineered monitoring setup. A proper observability stack - structured metrics, automated anomaly detection, alerting thresholds on key indicators like trade count - would have caught it within hours, not days. I didn't have one.

My wife was at the kitchen table when I came downstairs that morning, her laptop open to something she was reviewing for a client. She glanced up, read my face, and closed the lid.

"What happened?"

"The tests were passing."

"That's... good?"

"They were passing because nothing was running."

She sat back in her chair. "Go on."

"The backtest agent was executing against an empty date range. Zero trades. Zero results. The whole pipeline validated it as a success because there were no errors - just no data. Three days."

"Three days of green lights on an empty room." She said it slowly, like she was tasting how bad it was. "That's worse than a failure, isn't it? A failure you notice."

"Exactly. A failure screams at you. This just... smiled and waved."

She pulled her mug towards her, both hands wrapped around it. "I had something similar on the dashboard project last year. Remember? The health check endpoint that returned 200 OK for six weeks after the background worker died. The page looked fine. The data just stopped updating. Nobody noticed because the numbers on the screen were plausible - they were real numbers from six weeks ago."

"How'd you catch it?"

"A client rang and asked why their October data looked exactly like their September data." She half-smiled. "The monitoring was monitoring itself. The health check checked that the health check existed. Nobody had written a check for 'is the data actually fresh.'"

"So the test for 'does this work' wasn't testing 'does this work.'"

"Precisely. Which is obvious in hindsight and invisible in the moment." She tapped the edge of her laptop. "What are you going to do about it?"

The Observability Gap

AI agents aren't traditional pipelines. They don't fail cleanly. They fail *interpretively*.

When a bash command fails, it returns exit code 1. Clear. Observable.

When an AI agent "interprets" a requirement incorrectly, it returns valid code. Code that compiles. Code that runs. Code that does the wrong thing with the confidence of code doing the right thing.

The backtest agent didn't fail. It succeeded at running a backtest. The backtest just happened to have no trades because the date range was empty. The agent didn't know this was wrong. It did what it was told.

The failure wasn't in the execution. It was in the assumption. And assumptions don't throw exceptions.

What Needs Watching

After the three-day silent failure, I catalogued everything that needed observability. Three things mattered most.

The first was workflow health - not just "did it complete" but "did it complete meaningfully." Empty results need to be as loud as errors.

```
## Workflow Observability Checks

- [ ] Task started (timestamp, ticket ID, workflow
type)
- [ ] Context loaded (files read, tokens used,
time elapsed)
- [ ] Implementation complete (files changed,
lines added/removed)
- [ ] Tests run (count > 0, pass rate, coverage
delta)
- [ ] PR created (contains changes, not empty)
- [ ] Review passed (actual review, not skip)
```

The key is "count > 0." A test run that executes zero tests isn't a test run. A backtest with zero trades isn't a backtest. A PR with zero changes isn't a PR.

The second was token economics. Remember Chapter 9? The £150/month that constrains everything? You need to know where it's going.

```
## Token Observability
- Daily consumption by workflow type
- Consumption spikes (which task, which agent)
- Model tier distribution (Opus vs Sonnet vs
Haiku)
- Context efficiency (tokens per file read,
exploration vs retrieval)
```

The day I noticed 80% of my tokens going to a single agent that was stuck in an exploration loop, I saved myself from hitting the limit by 2 PM.

The third was agent decision points. When an agent makes a decision - which file to modify, which approach to take, which test to write - there should be a record. Not as a matter of trust, but because when something goes wrong, the decision log is where the answer lives.

```
## Decision Log: PROJ-456

10:14:32 - Approach selected: Modify existing
service (not create new)
10:14:45 - Files identified: [pricing_service.py,
tests/test_pricing.py]
10:15:02 - Implementation strategy: Add method to
existing class
10:18:33 - Test strategy: Unit tests + integration
test
10:22:15 - Coverage check: 94% -> 96% (acceptable)
10:23:01 - PR ready: All checks passed
```

Three weeks later, when someone asks "why did we add this method to PricingService instead of creating a new service?" the decision log has the answer.

The Dashboard That Doesn't Exist

I wanted a dashboard. A single screen showing all agent activity, all workflow states, all health metrics.

Such dashboards exist for traditional DevOps. Grafana. Datadog. New Relic. They don't exist for AI agent workflows. Not really. You can build them, but there's nothing off-the-shelf. This is a tooling gap that hasn't been filled yet - an entire category of software that the industry hasn't caught up to.

So I built something simpler. A log aggregator that I can actually read.

```
[2025-10-15 10:14:32] WORKFLOW:START ticket=PROJ-
456 type=dev-workflow
[2025-10-15 10:14:33] CONTEXT:LOAD files=12
tokens=15,234
[2025-10-15 10:14:45] DECISION:APPROACH
modify_existing=true reason="pattern_match"
[2025-10-15 10:18:33] TESTS:RUN count=7 passed=7
coverage=96%
[2025-10-15 10:23:01] PR:CREATE number=142
files_changed=2 lines_added=87
[2025-10-15 10:23:02] WORKFLOW:COMPLETE
duration=8m29s tokens_used=42,567

[2025-10-15 10:25:15] WORKFLOW:START ticket=PROJ-
457 type=dev-workflow
[2025-10-15 10:25:16] CONTEXT:LOAD files=3
tokens=4,221
[2025-10-15 10:30:00] TESTS:RUN count=0 passed=0
coverage=N/A
[2025-10-15 10:30:01] ALERT:EMPTY_TEST_RUN
ticket=PROJ-457 reason="no_test_files"
```

Line 10. That's what would have saved me three days. An alert that fires when tests run but nothing actually executes.

The log isn't pretty. It's not a dashboard. But it's greppable, which in practice means it's useful.

About two weeks after I set this up, the ALERT:EMPTY *TEST* RUN fired on a different ticket - PROJ-489, a refactoring task where the agent had reorganised the test directory structure and left the test runner pointed at the old path. I caught it in twelve minutes. Without the log, it would have been three more days of silence.

The Honest Bit

Here's what I should say plainly: the greppable log is a stopgap, not a solution.

I know this. I've known it since the three-day failure. A structured log with grep is fine for a single developer running a couple of scripts. It is not fine for a system running eight parallel agents across multiple repositories, processing financial data where silent errors have real consequences. The gap between what I have and what I need is not small.

What I need is a proper observability stack. Structured metrics piped into a time-series database. Automated anomaly detection that doesn't rely on me remembering to grep for the right thing each morning. Alerting thresholds that fire when trade counts drop to zero, when token consumption deviates from baselines, when an agent's output changes character in ways that suggest it's gone off the rails. Dashboards with graphs that make trends visible at a glance instead of buried in scrollback.

What I have is a text file and a terminal.

My wife asked about this after I'd described the PROJ-489 catch - the twelve-minute one that felt like a victory.

"So you caught it because you happened to be looking at the log?"

"The alert fired. I saw it."

"Where does the alert fire to?"

"The log."

She let that sit. "And you check the log how often?"

"Every morning. Sometimes midday."

"So if something breaks at two in the afternoon, the earliest you'd know is the next morning?"

"Unless I happened to be looking, yes."

"That's not an alert. That's a diary entry you read the next day."

I wanted to argue. But an alert that goes to a log file you check once a day is not an alert. It's a record. The PROJ-489 catch was lucky timing, not good engineering. The three-day backtest failure was the norm; the twelve-minute catch was the outlier.

So why haven't I built the proper thing? The honest answer is time and irony. Building a real observability stack - Prometheus, Grafana, custom exporters, alerting rules, the infrastructure to run it all - is a project in itself. Weeks of work, easily. And the whole point of this system is to ship features faster, not to spend a month building infrastructure to watch the infrastructure. There's a deep irony in putting the AI-assisted development project on hold so I can build a monitoring platform for the AI-assisted development project.

But irony doesn't change the fact that it's under-engineered. The greppable log was pragmatic for week one. It's a liability by month three. I haven't fixed this yet. I should.

The Alerts That Matter

Not everything needs an alert. Alert fatigue is real. If everything screams, nothing matters.

The filter is: "Would I want to know this immediately, or can it wait for the daily summary?"

Alert-worthy: - Test run with zero tests - PR with zero file changes - Workflow running for more than 30 minutes (stuck) - Token consumption spike (more than 2x normal for task type) - Contract validation failure - Review agent flagging blocking issues

Not alert-worthy: - Normal workflow completion - Expected test failures (flaky test, known issue) - Minor token variance - Documentation updates

The three-day failure? That's immediately. The agent completing a task successfully? That's daily summary.

The Audit Trail

This is how every workflow logs to a structured audit file

```
{
  "workflow_id": "wf-2025-10-15-001",
  "ticket": "PROJ-456",
  "type": "dev-workflow",
  "started_at": "2025-10-15T10:14:32Z",
  "completed_at": "2025-10-15T10:23:02Z",
  "status": "success",
  "decisions": [
    {
      "point": "approach_selection",
      "choice": "modify_existing",
      "alternatives": ["create_new",
"extend_base_class"],
      "reasoning": "Existing service matches 87%
of requirements"
    }
  ],
  "files_changed": ["pricing_service.py",
"tests/test_pricing.py"],
  "tests": {
    "count": 7,
    "passed": 7,
    "coverage_before": 94,
    "coverage_after": 96
  },
  "tokens": {
    "context": 15234,
    "generation": 27333,
    "total": 42567
  },
  "pr": {
    "number": 142,
    "url": "https://github.com/org/repo/pull/142"
```

```
    }
}
```

The principle is simple, alerts are for real-time awareness. Audit trails are for retrospective investigation.

When something goes wrong - not "if" but "when" - this audit trail is how I figure out what happened. Which decision led where. What the agent was thinking. Why the outcome occurred.

Without the trail, debugging agent behaviour is archaeology without artefacts. With the trail, it's reading a logbook.

The Human Checkpoint

Some things require human eyes. Not because agents can't handle them, but because the consequences of getting them wrong are too severe.

My checkpoint criteria:

1. **Production deployment.** Agent prepares. Human approves. Always.
2. **Database migrations.** Agent writes migration. Human reviews. Always.
3. **Security-sensitive changes.** Auth, permissions, encryption. Agent proposes. Human validates. Always.
4. **External API integrations.** Agent implements. Human tests against sandbox. Always.

5. **Financial calculations.** Agent writes logic. Human verifies against known-good examples. Always.

These aren't trust issues. They're risk management. The cost of agent error in these areas exceeds the cost of human review.

The observability system flags these checkpoints:

```
[2025-10-15 11:45:00] CHECKPOINT:REQUIRED
type=production_deploy
[2025-10-15 11:45:00] CHECKPOINT:WAITING
approval_needed=human
[2025-10-15 11:52:00] CHECKPOINT:APPROVED by=manju
duration=7m00s
[2025-10-15 11:52:01] DEPLOY:START
environment=production
```

The workflow pauses. The human reviews. The workflow continues. The audit trail records who approved what when.

The Meta-Observability Problem

Here's a recursion that bothered me: who watches the watching?

My wife brought it up before I did. We were on the sofa after the toddler went down, both half-watching something neither of us was following. I'd been describing the alert system - the heartbeat checks, the test alerts, the log rotation.

"So you've built a system to watch the agents," she said. "And now you're building a system to watch the system that watches the agents."

"And a cron job on a separate machine to watch *that*."

She turned to face me, tucking her legs underneath her. "Where does it end? Do you need a system to watch the cron job?"

"In theory, it's turtles all the way down. In practice, you stop when the cost of another layer exceeds the risk of the thing failing."

"But how do you know where that line is?"

I didn't have a neat answer. That was the honest truth. You make a judgement call. You pick a level of paranoia you can live with and accept that something, somewhere, could still fail silently.

"I don't, precisely," I said. "I know that the backtest agent failing silently cost me three days. I know the observability system failing silently would cost me more. So I watch the watcher. But the watcher's watcher is a cron job that sends me an email if it doesn't hear a heartbeat. If my email goes down, I'm in trouble. But at that point, I've got bigger problems than agent observability."

She thought about that. "It's like the smoke alarm thing. You check the battery in the smoke alarm. But you don't install a second smoke alarm to check the first one. At some point you just... accept that you've done enough."

"Unless you're me, apparently."

"Unless you're you." She picked up the remote, glanced at it, put it down again. "Can I ask you something? And I'm genuinely asking, not making a point."

"Go on."

"Are you watching the code, or are you watching yourself watch the code?"

I didn't answer immediately. It was a better question than she probably realised - or maybe she realised exactly how good it was. The observability infrastructure had taken ten hours to build. The daily review took fifteen minutes. But the mental overhead - the awareness that I needed to check the checks, verify the verifications - that was harder to measure. It was always running in the background, a thread I couldn't quite close.

"Both, probably," I said. "The system watches the agents. I watch the system. But I also watch myself to make sure I'm actually looking at what the system tells me and not just glancing at a green dashboard and assuming everything's fine."

"Which is what you were doing for three days before."

"Exactly."

She was quiet for a moment. "It's interesting. You used to come home stressed about bugs. Specific things. 'This API is returning the wrong data.' 'This view controller is leaking memory.' Now you come home stressed about... abstraction. Whether the thing you built to prevent stress is itself a source of stress."

"That's a bleak way to put it."

"It's an honest way to put it. I'm not saying it's bad. I'm saying it's different. The worry used to be concrete. Now it's meta."

The practical answer to the meta-observability problem is simpler than the philosophical one:

1. **Heartbeat check.** Every hour, the observability system logs that it's alive. If the heartbeat stops, something upstream notices.
2. **Test alert.** Every day, a scheduled task triggers a known-alertable condition. If the alert doesn't arrive, the alert system is broken.
3. **Log rotation verification.** Logs older than 7 days are archived. A check confirms the archive happened. If logs from last week don't exist, something's wrong.
4. **External watchdog.** A completely separate system - in my case, a cron job on a different machine - checks that the primary observability system is responsive.

It sounds excessive. A silent observability failure is worse than no observability at all - because you think you're watching when you're actually blind.

The Learning Loop

After a few weeks of logs, patterns began to surface - not from careful analysis, but from the kind of pattern recognition that happens when you stare at the same log format every morning. The numbers started telling a story.

```
## Observed Patterns (October 2025)

Token Usage:
```

```
- Dev workflows: avg 45,000 tokens (sigma =
12,000)
- PR reviews: avg 18,000 tokens (sigma = 5,000)
- Documentation updates: avg 8,000 tokens (sigma =
2,000)

Duration:
- Simple tickets: 8-15 minutes
- Medium tickets: 20-40 minutes
- Complex tickets: 60-120 minutes

Failure Modes:
- Empty test runs: 3 occurrences (all fixed by
adding assertion requirements)
- Token spikes: 2 occurrences (exploration loops)
- Contract violations: 5 occurrences (4 backend, 1
frontend)
```

These patterns inform improvements. The exploration loop incidents led to tighter context loading. The contract violations led to pre-implementation contract verification.

Without observability, I'd be guessing about what to improve. With it, I'm measuring.

The Trust Calibration

As the data accumulated, something shifted. I started trusting the agents more where they succeeded consistently, and less where patterns showed weakness.

High trust, based on data: test writing (zero escaped bugs in three months), code formatting (perfect consistency), PR creation (never missing files after workflow update), and documentation updates (always accurate).

Lower trust, also based on data: complex architecture decisions (3 "needed rework" incidents), performance optimisation (2 "made it worse" incidents), and legacy code changes (1 "broke production" incident).

The trust isn't emotional. It's statistical. The observability data tells me where agents excel and where they need supervision. The strange thing is what that felt like - trusting a machine not because I had a sense of its reliability, but because I had a spreadsheet of it.

My wife asked about this one evening. She'd been scrolling through her own project's error logs and overheard me say something about "high confidence in the test agent."

"What does it actually feel like?" she said. "Trusting something because of data instead of instinct?"

"Odd. Like trusting a stranger because you've read their credit report."

"You trust people on instinct all the time. Colleagues. Contractors. You've hired people based on a forty-five-minute conversation."

"That's different."

"Is it? You're making a judgement about capability based on limited information. The information's just in a different format." She turned her phone over in her hands. "I think what bothers me about it is that the data makes it feel more certain than it is. A spreadsheet looks definitive. Three months of clean test runs looks like proof. But it's still just a sample."

That observation nagged at me. Three months of success doesn't guarantee month four. The data reduces uncertainty. It doesn't eliminate it. I still check the things the data says I don't need to check - not every time, but often enough. Old habits, maybe. Or the reasonable suspicion that any system designed to make you feel safe is also designed to make you stop looking.

"You're less stressed about the robot stuff, though," she said. "I've noticed."

"I can see what they're doing now. Knowing what's happening is less stressful than imagining what might be happening."

"That's not a technology insight. That's just being a person."

"Most of the good insights are."

The Cost of Watching

Observability isn't free. There's overhead in computational terms (logging, aggregating, and alerting all take resources), in attention (someone has to review the daily summaries, investigate alerts, and maintain the system itself), and in complexity (more moving parts, more code to maintain).

My rough accounting:

- Setup: 10 hours
- Daily review: 15 minutes
- Maintenance: 2 hours per month
- Incident investigation: varies (but much faster with logs)

The return: zero three-day silent failures since implementation. Zero "when did this break?" mysteries. Zero "who approved this?" confusion.

Worth it.

Though my wife's question stayed with me longer than the numbers did. Am I watching the code, or watching myself watch the code? The answer, I suspect, is that the distinction matters less than the watching itself. Vigilance is vigilance, whether it's directed at a machine or at your own attention span. The real failure - the three-day kind, the kind that smiles and waves - happens when you stop asking the question at all.

CHAPTER 16

The Hard Limits

The Command That Almost Ran

"I'm going to delete the old configuration files to clean up the repository."

I read that line in the agent's output and felt my stomach drop. My hands moved faster than my thoughts - Ctrl+C, kill the process, stop everything.

The agent was about to run rm -rf config/legacy/. A perfectly reasonable cleanup. Except config/legacy/ contained configuration files critical to production that weren't backed up elsewhere. Legacy artefacts from a rushed deployment that nobody ever migrated properly because "it works."

Would the agent have actually deleted them? I don't know. I didn't let it try.

But the near-miss haunted me. A helpful cleanup suggestion, moments away from becoming an unrecoverable disaster.

That evening I sat down at the kitchen table and started writing rules. My wife was opposite me with her own laptop open, working through a client's React project.

"You're typing very aggressively for someone who isn't debugging," she said, without looking up.

"Writing rules for what the agents aren't allowed to do."

"Like Asimov?"

"Less philosophical. More 'never delete anything in config/ without asking first.'"

She glanced at my screen. "That seems like the kind of thing that shouldn't need writing down."

"For a human, no. For an agent that's trying to be helpful, everything needs writing down."

The Problem with Capability

AI agents are capable. That's the point. They can read files, write files, execute commands, make API calls, modify configurations.

A human developer has instincts. "This looks dangerous." "I should check with someone." "Let me back this up first." These instincts are trained through experience, usually painful experience.

AI agents don't have instincts. They have instructions. And if the instructions don't say "don't delete production credentials," the agent doesn't know not to delete production credentials.

The instincts need to be encoded. Explicitly. In rules that the agent cannot bypass.

The Guardrail Architecture

Guardrails operate at multiple levels, and I didn't design them in the abstract. I built them incident by incident, each layer added after something went wrong or almost did.

The first layer came the night of the config near-miss: a list of things that should never happen, under any circumstances.

```
## Forbidden Commands (NEVER execute)

- `rm -rf /` (obviously)
- `rm -rf` on any directory without explicit user
approval
- `DROP DATABASE` (any database)
- `TRUNCATE TABLE` on production
- `git push - force` to main/master
- Any command containing production credentials in
plaintext
- `chmod 777` (anything)
- Commands that disable security features
```

These aren't suggestions. The agent's execution layer checks every command against this list before running it. Match found? Refuse. Alert the human. Log the attempted violation.

The second layer came after the npm disaster - some things aren't forbidden, but they're dangerous enough to require human sign-off before they run.

```
## Approval Required (pause and ask)

- Any file deletion (rm, unlink, etc.)
- Database migrations (any ALTER, CREATE, DROP)
- Configuration changes in config/, .env files
- Changes to authentication/authorization code
- External API credential modifications
- Git operations affecting main branch
- Package dependency updates (npm, pip, cargo)
```

When an agent needs to do any of these, the workflow pauses. Human reviews. Human approves or rejects. Workflow continues or aborts.

The third layer addresses a subtler risk: some things are fine individually but dangerous in aggregate. An agent that wants to modify 200 files in one workflow probably isn't doing what you intended.

```
## Rate Limits

- File modifications: max 50 per workflow
- API calls to external services: max 100 per hour
- Database writes: max 1000 per workflow
- Git commits: max 10 per workflow
- Token consumption: max 100,000 per workflow
```

The rate limit catches runaway behaviour before it becomes runaway damage.

The fourth layer is scope. Agents should stay in their lane. A dev workflow agent working on a feature implementation doesn't need access to deployment configurations - so it doesn't get access, even if the code it's working on references deployment, even if it thinks updating the deployment config would be "helpful."

```
## Scope Boundaries

Dev workflow agent CAN:
- Modify files in src/
- Modify files in tests/
- Create files in src/ and tests/
- Run tests
- Create PRs

Dev workflow agent CANNOT:
- Modify files in config/
- Modify files in .github/
- Access production environments
```

```
- Deploy anything
- Modify CI/CD pipelines
```

Capability follows necessity. If you don't need it, you don't get it.

The Validation Layer

Guardrails are only as good as their enforcement. A rule that can be bypassed isn't a rule - it's a suggestion.

Every command, every file write, every API call passes through a validation layer before it reaches the system.

```
def execute_bash(command: str, context:
WorkflowContext) -> Result:
    # Check forbidden commands
    if is_forbidden(command):
        log_violation(command, context)
        return Result.blocked("Forbidden command")

    # Check approval requirements
    if requires_approval(command):
        approval = request_human_approval(command,
context)
        if not approval.granted:
            return Result.blocked("Human
rejected")

    # Check rate limits
    if exceeds_rate_limit(command, context):
        return Result.blocked("Rate limit
exceeded")

    # Check scope
    if outside_scope(command, context):
        return Result.blocked("Outside agent
```

```
scope")

    # All checks passed
    return actually_execute(command)
```

The agent never talks directly to the system. Everything goes through this layer. No exceptions. No "trusted mode." No "skip validation for simple commands."

Fail-Secure

When something goes wrong with the guardrail system itself, it fails closed.

If the validation layer can't determine whether a command is forbidden? Block it.

If the approval system is unreachable? Block the action.

If the rate limit database is corrupted? Block everything until it's fixed.

The default is "no." The only way to "yes" is through explicit validation.

The Bypass Temptation

Sometimes the guardrails feel inconvenient. The agent wants to do something sensible. The guardrail blocks it. The human knows it's fine.

"Can't I just... disable the check this one time?"

No. The moment you create a bypass mechanism, you create a vulnerability. Every bypass is a hole in the fence. One hole is enough.

When the guardrail is wrong, there are legitimate responses: adjust the rule for all cases, not just this one. Do it manually - some things should require human action. Or expand the scope definition through the proper change process. Not a bypass - a deliberate expansion.

"But it's just this once" is how every security breach starts.

The Incident That Shaped the Rules

The near-miss with the config directory wasn't the only one. There were others. Each one added a rule.

The package.json incident:

An agent wanted to "update dependencies for security." It ran npm update. All dependencies updated to latest. Including three major version bumps that broke the entire application.

Rule added: Dependency updates require explicit human approval. No blanket updates.

The database migration incident:

An agent created a migration that added an index. Reasonable. The index took hours to build on the production dataset because the table was significantly larger than anyone expected.

Rule added: Database migrations on tables larger than 1 million rows require impact assessment and human approval.

The git history incident:

An agent wanted to "clean up commit history" and ran an interactive rebase that squashed a month of commits into three. Lost all the granular context.

Rule added: Git history modification commands are forbidden. Period.

The credentials-in-logs incident:

An agent was debugging an API issue and logged request details that included sensitive information. To a file that nearly got committed to the repository.

Rule added: Any log statement is scanned for credential patterns before execution. Matches get blocked and flagged.

Each rule exists because something bad happened, or almost happened. The guardrails aren't theoretical. They're scar tissue.

The Allowlist vs Blocklist Debate

There are two approaches to guardrails: define what's forbidden and allow everything else (a blocklist), or define what's permitted and forbid everything else (an allowlist).

For AI agents, I've landed on a hybrid. Capabilities use an allowlist - an agent can only do what it's explicitly permitted to do, and if it's not in the scope definition, it's not on the table. Within those allowed capabilities, dangerous patterns use a blocklist - the rm -rf without confirmation, the force push to main.

The allowlist catches unknown unknowns. The blocklist catches known dangers with extra clarity. An agent allowed to "modify files in src/" with a blocklist rule against "deleting files without approval" has two layers of protection: it can't delete files outside src/ (allowlist), and it can't delete files inside src/ without asking (blocklist).

Belt and braces.

The Human Override

Sometimes the guardrails are actually wrong. Not "inconvenient" - wrong. There's a human override for this. But it's intentionally inconvenient: explicit acknowledgment of which rule and why, written justification logged permanently, a post-override review to determine if the rule needs updating, and visibility in the daily report.

The friction is the point. Overrides should be rare, deliberate, and documented. If you're overriding constantly, your rules are wrong and need fixing - not bypassing.

In practice? I've used the override twice in six months. Both times led to rule improvements.

The Trust Gradient

Not all agents need the same guardrails. A test-runner that only runs tests needs minimal constraints. A deployment agent that pushes to production needs maximum constraints - every action logged, every significant step approved.

The trust gradient:

```
- Test Runner → Minimal guardrails (limited
capabilities anyway)
- Code Reviewer → Light guardrails (read-only,
suggestions only)
- Dev Workflow → Moderate guardrails (can write,
but scoped)
- DB Migrator → Heavy guardrails (dangerous
capabilities)
- Deployer → Maximum guardrails (production
access)
```

Guardrails scale with blast radius. If an agent can only affect local files, loose rules are fine. If an agent can affect production, tight rules are mandatory.

The Security Blind Spot

All those guardrails - the forbidden commands, the approval gates, the rate limits, the scope boundaries - they share a common assumption. They assume the danger is in what the agent *does*. Delete a file. Drop a table. Force-push to main. Operational disasters. Visible, immediate, catastrophic.

But there's a category of harm they don't touch at all: the code the agent writes.

I discovered this the way I discover most things. Painfully.

The agent was implementing a log-viewing feature for the dashboard. Simple enough: fetch logs from the database, filter by job ID, return them to the frontend. The code it produced was clean. Well-structured. Proper error handling. It passed every test.

During a manual review - one of those late-evening sessions where you're scrolling through diffs with half your attention - I noticed the database query. String concatenation. The job ID, taken directly from the request parameter, interpolated straight into the SQL string.

The query:

```
query = f"SELECT * FROM job_logs WHERE job_id =
'{job_id}'"
```

Classic SQL injection. A textbook vulnerability. The kind they teach you about in the first week of any security course. And the agent had written it without hesitation, because nothing in the guardrails said "don't write injectable SQL." The guardrails stopped the agent from *dropping* the database. They didn't stop it from writing code that would let an attacker do it instead.

I went back through recent PRs with fresh eyes and a sinking feeling. Most of the code was fine. But I found a JWT stored in localStorage instead of an httpOnly cookie - visible to any XSS attack. A CORS configuration set to allow all origins. An API endpoint returning full user objects, passwords hashed but present, because the agent had mapped the database model directly to the response without filtering fields.

None of these triggered a single guardrail. Every one of them was a security vulnerability hiding behind syntactically perfect code.

My wife noticed the expression on my face. She was working on something of her own - a Next.js project for a client in healthcare.

"What's wrong?"

"The agent's been writing insecure code and I've been approving it."

She put her laptop down. "How insecure?"

"SQL injection. Exposed tokens. The greatest hits." I rubbed my face. "The thing is, the code *looks* good. It's well-organised, it follows the patterns, it handles errors gracefully. It just also happens to be exploitable."

"I had the same thing last month," she said. "An AI-generated auth flow that looked beautiful. Stored the refresh token in a cookie without the Secure flag. Would've worked fine in development. In production, over HTTP during a redirect, that token's flying across the wire in plaintext."

"Did you catch it?"

"My linter caught the cookie flag. But only because someone had written a custom rule for exactly that pattern. If it had been a slightly different vulnerability - something the linter didn't know about - no."

That was the uncomfortable truth. I could add rules to the CLAUDE.md: always use parameterised queries, never store tokens in localStorage, never return password fields in API responses, always set Secure and httpOnly on auth cookies. And I did add those rules. The review agent got a security checklist too - a set of patterns to scan for in every PR.

But it's pattern-matching against known vulnerabilities. It catches the SQL injection because SQL injection is famous. It catches the localStorage JWT because that's a well-documented anti-pattern. It won't catch the subtle authorisation bypass that doesn't match any checklist item. It won't catch the timing side-channel in the comparison function. It won't catch the business logic flaw that lets a user access another user's data through a perfectly valid-looking API call.

The guardrails prevent the agent from burning the house down. They don't prevent it from leaving the windows unlocked.

I added a section to the daily report: security-relevant changes flagged for manual review. Any PR that touches authentication, authorisation, database queries, or external API calls gets extra scrutiny. It's not automated protection - it's a reminder to pay attention to the things automation can't reliably catch.

Another scar. Another rule. But this time, a rule with a footnote: *this is necessary but not sufficient.*

That footnote nagged at me. "Necessary but not sufficient" is the kind of phrase you write to sound wise and then move on. I didn't want to move on. The blind spot had properly rattled me - not the SQL injection itself, which was fixable, but the realisation that my entire safety architecture had a category-shaped hole in it. The guardrails were operational. The code the agent produced was unguarded.

So I did what I always do when something scares me enough: I researched until the fear became specific.

SAST tools - Static Application Security Testing. Semgrep, SonarQube, Bandit. Tools that scan source code for known vulnerability patterns, the way a spell checker scans for misspellings. I'd been vaguely aware they existed. I'd never set one up. That weekend, I installed Semgrep, pointed it at the last three months of PRs, and waited.

It found things. An insecure deserialisation pattern in a webhook handler - the agent had used pickle.loads on data from an external source, which is roughly equivalent to running eval() on user input. A path traversal vulnerability in a file upload handler where the filename from the request was joined directly to the storage path without sanitisation. Neither of these had been flagged by my review agent. Neither had been caught in my manual reviews. They'd been sitting in the codebase for weeks.

Semgrep also produced false positives. A flagged "hardcoded password" that was actually a test fixture. A "potential ReDoS" on a regex that was only ever applied to system-generated strings. Triaging these took time. But the ratio was instructive: for every three false positives, there was one genuine finding that nobody - human or AI - had caught through normal review.

The key insight wasn't that SAST replaces human review. It's that SAST and human review are different lenses looking at the same code. My review agent catches logic problems - wrong algorithm, missed edge case, poor error handling. The SAST tool catches security patterns - injection, deserialisation, path traversal. Neither catches everything. Together they cover more ground than either alone.

Dependency scanning was the next rabbit hole. The npm update incident had taught me about direct dependencies - don't blindly update, audit first, npm audit exists for a reason. But AI-generated code introduces a subtler problem. The agent doesn't just pull in libraries. It pulls in *patterns* it learned from training data, including patterns that reference libraries with known vulnerabilities. Sometimes npm auditcatches the dependency. But sometimes the agent writes code that mimics a vulnerable pattern without importing the library that would trigger the scanner. A ghost vulnerability - the shape of the security hole without the dependency that would set off alarms.

My wife had a version of this. Copilot had suggested a regex for email validation in her healthcare project. It looked fine. It compiled. It matched valid emails. It was also vulnerable to ReDoS - catastrophic backtracking on certain malformed inputs that could pin a CPU at 100% for minutes. No vulnerable dependency to flag. Just a vulnerable pattern the model had learned from training data somewhere, reproduced without context or warning.

That's the supply-chain problem, and it's the one I still don't have a clean answer for. When a human writes code, the supply chain is straightforward: developer writes code, code goes to production. When an AI writes code, the supply chain includes the model's entire training corpus - every open-source project, every Stack Overflow answer, every tutorial with a security bug that the model absorbed and learned to reproduce. You're not just reviewing one developer's work. You're reviewing the distilled habits of millions of developers, including their worst habits, filtered through a model that can't distinguish between a pattern that's popular because it's good and a pattern that's popular because it was copy-pasted from a blog post written in 2014 by someone who didn't know better.

I added "treat AI-generated code as untrusted input" to my CLAUDE.md as a principle. Whether that actually changes my review behaviour - whether I review AI-generated code with genuinely more suspicion than I review my own - I'm honest enough to admit it mostly doesn't. The principle is correct. My discipline is inconsistent.

Here's where I landed. Semgrep runs as part of the PR review pipeline now, alongside the review agent. Every dependency change triggers npm audit. The review agent has its security checklist. The daily report flags security-relevant changes. I'm aware of the supply-chain problem even if I haven't solved it.

It's not a proactive security posture. A proper one would include DAST - Dynamic Application Security Testing, actually running the application and probing it for vulnerabilities - and regular penetration testing, and a formal threat model. I haven't done any of that. What I have is reactive-plus: better than purely reactive, not yet proactive. The windows aren't all locked. But I've at least walked through the house and made a list of which ones are open.

Another item for the list of things I know I should do better but haven't. The list is long. It keeps growing. That's probably the most honest thing I can say about security in an AI-assisted workflow: knowing the shape of what you don't know is itself a form of progress, even if it doesn't feel like enough.

Constraints as a Form of Love

By the time the guardrail system was mature - four layers deep, every rule traceable to a specific incident - I'd spent what felt like an unreasonable number of hours telling software what it wasn't allowed to do.

My wife was at the kitchen counter, reviewing a PR from one of her client's junior developers, while I sat at the table working through yet another refinement to the scope boundaries.

"You've been at this for a while," she said, not looking up from her screen. "How many rules is it now?"

"Depends how you count. Forbidden commands, approval gates, rate limits, scope boundaries - maybe sixty or seventy distinct constraints across all the agents."

"Seventy rules." She let out a low whistle. "You're spending a lot of time telling the robots what they're not allowed to do."

"Constraints are a form of love."

She looked up from her screen properly. "That's either profound or very strange."

"Think about it. You constrain things you care about. Gates at the top of stairs. Locks on medicine cabinets. Not because the child is malicious - because they don't understand consequences yet."

"The agents aren't children, Manju."

"No, but the principle's the same. The guardrails aren't there because I don't trust the agents. They're there because I trust them to do exactly what I tell them - including the destructive things I didn't mean to tell them."

She turned on her stool to face me. "I had a junior developer last year. Smart, really sharp. First week, she refactored the authentication module - cleaned up the code beautifully, removed what she thought was dead logic. Except it was the session timeout handler. Logged out every user on the platform."

"Ouch."

"The code was technically better after her change. But she didn't have the context to know what she was removing. So I put her on a branch protection rule. Every PR to the auth module needed my sign-off. She thought I was punishing her." She paused. "She didn't really understand until she reviewed someone else's PR that nearly dropped an index on the users table. Then the gates made sense."

"Exactly. You don't add constraints because someone is bad at their job. You add them because some mistakes aren't recoverable."

"Right. But here's my question." She picked up her tea. "Are all seventy of your rules actually necessary? Or have some of them become security theatre?"

I didn't answer immediately.

"Something goes wrong, you add a rule," she continued. "Something else goes wrong, another rule. Eventually the agents spend half their time asking permission to do things that are perfectly fine."

"I've only overridden twice in six months."

"Which is either discipline or a sign they're too constrained to be useful." She sipped her tea. "Do you ever review the rules themselves? Delete the ones that don't earn their keep?"

The rate limit on git commits - ten per workflow. I'd added it early. In practice, no workflow had ever hit five. The rule existed. It had never done anything.

"Some of them are probably redundant," I admitted.

"Keep the ones that have actually blocked something real. The config protection, the force-push ban, the credential scanning - those have teeth. A rate limit on commits that nobody's ever hit is just noise."

"Cheap noise, though."

"It costs attention. And attention is the thing you keep telling me is your actual scarce resource."

I didn't have a good counter-argument, which is usually how I know I need to listen.

"There's a parenting version of this," she said. "When he was fourteen months, we had safety locks on every cupboard in the kitchen. Every single one. And he screamed every time he wanted his water cup because it was behind a locked door."

"I remember."

"So we took the locks off the cupboard with his cups and plates. Left them on the ones with the cleaning products and the knives. Same child. Same kitchen. Fewer locks. More appropriate locks."

I looked at my guardrail configuration file. Seventy rules. Some load-bearing. Some left over from early paranoia, from before I knew which mistakes the agents would actually make versus which ones I'd imagined they might.

"I'll do a review," I said. "Trim the ones that have never fired."

"Keep the scar tissue," she said. "Bin the hypotheticals."

The Living Document

The guardrails aren't static. They evolve.

Every incident adds a rule. Every false positive triggers a review. Every override prompts the question: was the rule wrong? And now, periodically, rules that have never fired get scrutinised: real risk, or imagined one?

```
## Guardrail Changelog

2025-07-15: Added rm-rf confirmation requirement
2025-07-18: Expanded forbidden commands to include
DROP DATABASE
2025-08-01: Added rate limit for file
modifications (50 per workflow)
2025-08-03: Added credential pattern scanning for
logs
2025-08-10: Relaxed npm install restriction (allow
exact versions)
2025-08-14: Added scope boundaries for deployment
agent
2025-09-01: Removed commit rate limit (never
triggered, redundant with PR limits)
```

The changelog is part of the documentation. When someone asks "why can't I do X?" the changelog has the answer. Usually a story. Usually a painful one. "2025-08-03: Added credential pattern scanning for logs" - something happened on 2025-08-02. The changelog records the lesson; the fear that generated it lives just behind each date.

And now, some entries record removals too. A mature guardrail system isn't one that only grows. It's one that prunes.

The Final Layer

After all the guardrails, after all the validation, there's one final layer: the human who's paying attention.

Observability shows what's happening. Guardrails prevent the worst. But human awareness catches the things that rules can't anticipate.

The three-day silent failure from Chapter 15? No guardrail could have prevented that. It wasn't doing anything wrong. It was doing the right thing with wrong data. Human attention caught it. Eventually. Not fast enough, but eventually.

The automation enables the attention. By handling the routine, by enforcing the rules, by catching the predictable - the automation frees humans to watch for the unpredictable.

The hard limits make the soft attention possible.

CHAPTER 17

The Oversight Economy

The Job That Changed Shape

Fifteen years ago, I wrote code for a living. Every character, every function, every algorithm - my fingers, my brain, my craft.

Now? I write instructions for systems that write code. I review output. I approve changes. I configure workflows that run without me.

The job description didn't change. The job did.

Some days I feel like a fraud. I shipped three features today. I wrote perhaps fifty lines of code myself. The rest was AI, executing my instructions, following my patterns, implementing my specifications.

Is that my work? Is it our work? Is it something new that doesn't have a name yet?

The productivity metrics say yes. The features shipped. The tests pass. The clients are happy. By every measurable outcome, the work is getting done.

But the *doing* of it feels different. And I'm not sure that feeling has a name either.

What I Actually Do Now

If I'm honest about the shape of my day: mornings go to reviewing overnight agent output - what completed, what failed, where something looks off. Then ticket triage, which is architecture work, not implementation work. Then direct sessions for the complex problems, the back-and-forth with the AI that feels less like using a tool and more like arguing with a very fast, very literal junior who occasionally produces something brilliant. Afternoons: PRs coming in, read the changes, check the requirements, approve or push back. Late afternoons: process work - what went wrong yesterday, what guardrail is stale, what documentation nobody updated.

It's management. That's the uncomfortable truth. I manage AI systems the way a team lead manages developers. Set direction. Review output. Handle escalations. Improve processes.

I didn't set out to become a manager. I liked writing code. I was good at it. The transition happened gradually, then suddenly. The tools got better. The leverage increased. The equation tipped.

Now I manage robots. And I'm not sure how to feel about that.

The Oversight Economy

Here's the model that finally made sense to me, though it's cleaner in theory than in practice.

The old economy ran on skill multiplied by time. Eight hours is eight hours.

The new economy runs on oversight multiplied by leverage. The constraint isn't time - it's attention. The quality of your watching.

I call it the oversight economy. The scarce resource isn't human labour. It's human judgement.

The agents can generate unlimited code. They can parallelise across infinite instances. What they can't do is judge whether the code is *right*. Not architecturally right. Not business-logic right. Not "fits our specific weird requirements" right.

That judgement is human. For now. Maybe forever.

The job isn't "write code." The job is "ensure the right code gets written." Oversight.

The Skills That Matter

Some skills became more valuable. Specification clarity is the obvious one - if you can't explain what you want precisely, you can't get what you want from AI. Vague in, vague out, and the vagueness is now wearing a confident face.

Pattern recognition matters more now than it ever did when I was writing code myself. Reading a hundred lines of generated code and sensing that it's subtly off - not broken, not yet, but heading somewhere that will hurt in six months. The instinct is harder to maintain when you're reviewing instead of building, because building teaches you where the problems live.

System thinking became the whole game. And review speed became the bottleneck I didn't anticipate. The AI outpaces my review capacity on bad weeks, which means the queue backs up and I start rubber-stamping things I should be reading more carefully. That's where things go wrong.

What matters less: typing speed, syntax memory, implementation details. The mechanical knowledge that used to differentiate developers is now available to anyone who can ask. Something was lost in that. I'm still deciding what.

The Existential Question

My wife asked me on a Thursday evening.

We were on the sofa, the toddler finally down after a forty-minute negotiation that had involved two stories, one glass of water, and a philosophical debate about why the moon doesn't fall. She had her laptop open on one knee, client code on screen - a React dashboard she'd been refactoring all week with Copilot doing most of the heavy lifting. I had mine closed. I'd been staring at the wall for about ten minutes, which is how she knew something was wrong.

"What do you actually *do* then?"

She'd been reading a draft of this book. Not the whole thing - the first handful of chapters, the ones about prompts and protocols and the elaborate infrastructure I'd built. She'd read them the way she reads code: carefully, looking for the logic underneath.

"What do you mean?"

"I mean - " She closed her own laptop and turned to face me properly. "You describe all these systems. The agents write the code. The agents run the tests. The agents do the reviews. You've got workflows for everything. So what's left? What's the actual *you* part?"

"Everything important."

"That's not an answer. That's a slogan."

She wasn't being cruel. She was doing what she always does when something doesn't parse - pulling on the thread until the logic either holds or unravels.

"I decide what to build," I said. "I design the architecture. I set the constraints. I review the output and catch the things the AI misses."

"Right. So you're a manager."

"It's not management."

"You set direction, review output, handle escalations, and improve processes. That's the job description of every engineering manager I've ever worked with."

I didn't say anything for a moment. She picked at a loose thread on the sofa cushion, waiting.

"Does that bother you?" she asked. "Being a manager?"

"I didn't become a developer to be a manager. I became a developer because I liked building things."

"Do you still build things?"

"I... direct the building of things."

"That's what I thought." She pulled her feet up underneath her. "I've been having the same problem, you know. Not with your project. With mine."

I hadn't expected that. "What do you mean?"

"Last Tuesday I had Copilot generate an entire data visualisation component. Charts, tooltips, responsive layouts, accessibility labels - the lot. Took about twenty minutes. The old me would have spent a day and a half on it. Maybe two."

"And?"

"And it was good. Actually good. Not just functional - the code was clean, the patterns were solid. Better than what I'd have written under time pressure, if I'm honest." She paused. "I spent the rest of the afternoon reviewing it. Making small adjustments. Checking edge cases. And I kept thinking: is this still my work? My name's going on the invoice. But the thing I'm billing for isn't the thing I trained to do."

"What are you billing for?"

"Judgement, I suppose. Knowing that the responsive breakpoints the AI chose won't work for the client's user base. Knowing that the tooltip positioning will break on mobile Safari because it always breaks on mobile Safari."

"That sounds like what I do."

"I know. That's what worries me."

The room was quiet for a bit. From upstairs, the monitor crackled with the sound of the toddler turning over in his sleep.

"Do you actually still enjoy it?" she asked.

I wanted to say yes immediately. The way you say yes when someone asks if you're fine - automatic, defensive, not really an answer. But she'd know.

"Parts of it," I said. "The architecture work. The complex sessions where I'm going back and forth with Claude and something clicks. Those still feel like building."

"And the rest?"

"The rest feels like watching. Approving. Making sure nothing goes wrong. It's important work. But it's not why I fell in love with coding."

She was quiet again. Not the comfortable quiet of two people who've run out of things to say. The taut quiet of two people sitting with something they'd rather not be sitting with.

"I worry about my hands," she said.

"Your hands?"

"Not literally. But - I used to build a component from scratch. CSS, JSX, state management, the lot. Start from nothing, end with something. Now I start by asking the AI to scaffold it, and I shape what comes back. It's faster. It's probably better. But I'm not building from nothing anymore. I'm editing something."

"That's still skill."

"I know it's still skill. But it's a different skill. And I don't know if the one I'm losing is the one I'll need later." She looked at me. "What if the judgement depends on the building? What if you can only evaluate code properly if you've recently written it yourself?"

I'd thought about this. The skill atrophy question. I'd written about it, even - a line about the instinct being harder to maintain. But hearing her say it with genuine worry rather than theoretical concern made it land differently.

"I don't know," I said.

"That's not reassuring."

"No. It's not."

She picked up her cold tea from the coffee table, looked at it, put it back down. "We're both doing this, you know. Handing over more of the actual making to the machines and telling ourselves the thinking is the valuable part. But what if we're wrong? What if the thinking was always downstream of the making?"

"Then we're in trouble."

"Then everyone's in trouble. Not just us." She turned her tea mug in circles on the table. "What about the juniors? The people who never got fifteen years of building to fall back on? If the path to judgement runs through years of implementation, and implementation is being automated away - where does judgement come from?"

I didn't have an answer. The question sat between us on the sofa, heavy and unresolved.

"Are you scared?" she asked.

"Sometimes. Are you?"

"More than sometimes." She said it simply, without drama. "I had a call with a client on Monday. They asked if they could reduce the team from four developers to two, now that AI tools are - their words - 'handling more of the workload.' They weren't being hostile. They were doing maths."

"What did you tell them?"

"That the tools increase output, they don't replace judgement. The same thing everyone in our position says." She paused. "I believe it. Mostly. But 'mostly' is doing a lot of work in that sentence."

I reached over and took her cold tea, drank some of it myself. It was terrible.

"I keep coming back to that demo," I said. "Chapter one. The four-minute video. The fear. I thought I'd processed it. Built all these systems, wrote all these protocols. Turned the fear into infrastructure."

"And?"

"And the fear's still there. Underneath everything. I just built very elaborate furniture on top of it."

She almost smiled. "Protocols as coping mechanisms."

"Don't put it like that."

"Why not? It's honest." She uncurled from the sofa and stood up. "I don't think there's an answer tonight. I think we're both going to keep doing this - building with AI, reviewing AI output, telling ourselves the human part matters - because it does matter, and because we don't have a better option, and because the mortgage exists regardless of our existential crises."

"That's bleak."

"It's Tuesday."

She collected her laptop and her cold tea. At the doorway she stopped.

"For what it's worth, I don't think you're a fraud. I think the job changed, and you changed with it, and it's okay to not know what to call the thing you've become. I don't know what to call mine either."

She went upstairs. I sat in the dark for a while, the way I had that first night six months ago, except now instead of watching a demo on repeat I was staring at a blank wall and thinking about the distance between the developer I'd trained to be and the developer I'd become.

The fear from Chapter 1 wasn't gone. It had just changed shape. Become something quieter, less acute, more permanent. Not the sharp terror of obsolescence, but the low hum of uncertainty - the kind you learn to work alongside because it doesn't go away.

Keeping the Hands Warm

That question - *what if the judgement depends on the building?* - stayed with me. Not as a background hum. As an itch.

So I started a practice. Twice a week, usually early morning before the agents have anything for me to review, I write code by hand. No AI. No Copilot. No Claude. Just me, a blank file, and a problem.

Small things, mostly. A utility function. A data parser. A tricky bit of state management I'd normally hand off. The kind of code the AI could produce in thirty seconds and I now take forty minutes to write.

It's humbling. My fingers have forgotten things. I reach for syntax I used daily two years ago and it's gone, evaporated like a word on the tip of your tongue. I find myself wanting to ask Claude "what's the method for..." and having to stop, open the documentation myself, read it the way I used to - slowly, linearly, without a summariser in between.

The code I produce in these sessions is worse than what the AI would write. Slower. Buggier. Less idiomatic. I once spent twenty minutes debugging a state update that turned out to be a missing dependency in a useEffect array. Claude would have got that right first time.

But something happens during those sessions that doesn't happen when I'm reviewing AI output. My brain re-engages with the *texture* of code. The way a function fits into its context. The weight of a dependency choice. When I go back to reviewing agent output afterwards, I catch things I'd have missed. The calibration resets.

My wife noticed. "You're writing code again," she said one morning, looking over my shoulder at something distinctly amateurish on my screen.

"Keeping the hands warm."

She nodded slowly. "Like a pianist doing scales."

"Exactly like that."

The Control Group

She didn't adopt my system, incidentally. I'd half-expected her to. The CLAUDE.md files, the contract-first approach, the agent orchestration - it's all transferable. But she watched me build it, read the chapters about it, and chose a different path entirely.

Her relationship with Copilot is conversational, not structural. She uses it the way you'd use a very knowledgeable colleague sitting next to you - ask, receive, adjust. No elaborate protocols. No multi-agent pipelines. No 262-line instruction files governing agent behaviour.

It took a specific Saturday morning for me to understand what that actually meant in practice.

We were both working. Not unusual - freelance life means weekends blur. The toddler was at my parents' place for a few hours, and we'd both seized the quiet the way you seize a life raft. She was at the dining table. I was in the study. Separate rooms, separate clients, separate problems. She had a notification system to build for a client's React app - user preferences, channel routing, the usual. I had an API integration layer for a new data source, roughly equivalent complexity.

I started the way I always start. Read the EXISTENCE_MANIFEST. Checked the API contracts. Loaded the relevant service documentation. Set up the agent workspace - isolated branch, shallow clone, the full protocol. Wrote the specification: here's the endpoint, here's the contract, here's the expected behaviour, here are the edge cases. Configured the agent orchestration. Kicked off the first pass. Reviewed. Pushed back on a normalisation pattern. Second pass. Better. Wrote tests against the contract, not the implementation. Ran them. Two failures, both legitimate. Traced both back to a type mismatch in the producer. Fixed the producer. Green.

Solid work. Thorough. I was making coffee in the kitchen around half eleven when she wandered in, stretching.

"Done?" I asked.

"Shipped twenty minutes ago. You?"

I hadn't shipped yet. I was perhaps forty minutes from done. I'd been working since half eight, same as her. Three hours in, she was finished and I wasn't.

"Nearly," I said. "Just running the final checks."

She poured herself a glass of water and leaned against the counter. "I could hear you muttering. Sounded intense."

"I was arguing with an agent about a normalisation layer."

"Did you win?"

"The codebase won. Which is the point."

She raised an eyebrow but didn't push it. I went back and finished up. By the time I shipped, she'd moved on to a second task entirely.

Here's what I know about those two pieces of work, because I looked later. My integration had full test coverage - unit, integration, contract tests. Type-safe end to end. The agent workspace protocol meant zero risk of conflicting with other work. The specification was documented. If anyone needed to extend it in six months, the intent would be obvious.

Hers worked. Clean, functional, well-structured. Standard test coverage - the kind Copilot suggests and she supplements with the cases she knows matter. No specification document. No contract tests. No agent workspace. If someone needed to extend it in six months, they'd read the code, which was readable, because she writes readable code.

Both clients were happy. Both pieces of work were professional. Neither had bugs in production.

Hers was done forty minutes faster.

I brought it up a few weeks later. We were walking to the park - the long route, past the allotments, the one we take when the toddler's in the pushchair and might actually nap. One of those bright, sharp mornings where the cold is clean rather than miserable.

"Can I ask you something about your Copilot setup?"

"You want to know why I don't use your system."

"I want to understand the tradeoff."

She walked for a bit, thinking about it properly rather than giving me the quick answer. I appreciate that about her. She treats questions about her work the same way she treats questions about architecture - with the seriousness they deserve.

"Your system is brilliant," she said. "It's also yours. I'd be maintaining your infrastructure instead of building my own instincts."

"But the infrastructure catches things. The contract-first approach, the agent protocols - they prevent entire categories of mistakes."

"They prevent your categories of mistakes." She steered the pushchair around a puddle. "You build systems because you think in systems. The CLAUDE.md, the pre-code checklist, the existence manifest - that's how your brain works. You externalise your discipline into documentation because that's what makes you feel safe."

"It's not about feeling safe. It's about catching things before they become problems."

"Right. And when something breaks in my setup, I know where to look, because my setup has about four moving parts. When something breaks in yours, you have to work out which layer of the protocol failed.

That's not better or worse. It's a different debugging surface."

That landed somewhere uncomfortable. My system has layers. Layers are good - they catch things at different stages. But layers are also complexity, and complexity has a maintenance cost that I'd been accounting for in hours but not in cognitive overhead.

"So you think the protocol is unnecessary?"

"I think the protocol is necessary for you. I genuinely do. You're building something with six microservices and a trading engine. You need orchestration. You need contracts. The scale demands it." She paused. "But you also use the same protocol for a thirty-line utility function. That's not scale-appropriate. That's habit."

I wanted to argue. The protocol is the protocol. You don't skip the pre-flight checklist on a short flight.

But she wasn't saying skip it. She was saying her aircraft was a different size.

"What do you lose without it?" I asked.

"Coverage, probably. My tests are good but yours are better. Documentation - I write less, which will cost me eventually. Reproducibility - you could hand your codebase to another developer tomorrow. Mine would take more onboarding."

"What do you gain?"

"Forty minutes on a Saturday morning." She smiled. "And a simpler mental model. I hold the whole thing in my head. You hold it in documents. Both work. Mine is faster. Yours is more resilient."

We walked in silence for a bit. The toddler had fallen asleep, which meant we had perhaps twenty minutes of adult conversation left before the nap ended and diplomacy resumed.

"Do you think I over-engineered it?" I asked.

She took a long time to answer. Long enough that I heard two separate birds, a distant lawnmower, and someone's dog barking at a squirrel.

"I think you built exactly the system that someone with your brain and your project and your anxieties would build. And it works. It genuinely works - the results in your codebase are better than anything you'd have produced without it." She glanced at me. "But I also think that if you handed that system to ten developers, three would thrive with it, three would strip it back to the parts that matter, and four would drown in the overhead. It's a methodology. It's also a personality test."

The uncomfortable question, the one the Pragmatic Programmer review identified, the one I'd been circling for months: is the 262-line CLAUDE.md essential infrastructure, or is it me? Am I an infrastructure builder because the problem demands infrastructure, or because building infrastructure is what I do when I'm uncertain? Did I create the oversight economy, or did I create an elaborate coping mechanism that happens to produce good software?

I don't know.

That's not false modesty. I genuinely cannot separate the methodology from the temperament. I build systems. She builds instincts. Both approaches produce professional work. Both have failure modes - mine fails through complexity, hers through under-specification. Neither of us has had a production incident that the other's approach would have prevented.

The evidence is inconclusive. The sample size is two. And one of the samples is writing the book, which introduces a bias so obvious it barely needs stating.

What I believe, on my better days: the principles matter. Contract-first development catches real bugs. Specification clarity reduces waste. Oversight discipline prevents the kind of slow codebase decay that kills projects over months. These are not personality traits. They are engineering practices with measurable outcomes.

What I suspect, on my honest days: the implementation of those principles - the specific, elaborate, obsessively maintained infrastructure I built around them - is at least partly temperamental. The principles could live in a lighter system. They could live in her system, even, absorbed as instincts rather than codified as protocols.

She does contract-first development. She just doesn't write it down. She does specification clarity. She just holds it in her head instead of a manifest. The discipline is the same. The externalisation is different.

Maybe the book should have been shorter. Maybe the methodology is three principles and everything else is scaffolding.

I haven't resolved this. I'm not going to resolve it here, in the final chapter, with a neat epiphany that makes everything cohere. The discomfort is the point. If you build a system and it works, and someone else doesn't use your system and their work also works, you have to sit with the possibility that you built something for yourself and called it universal.

I believe the system matters. I cannot prove it would matter for her. That's where I've left it.

The Productivity Paradox

I'm more productive than I've ever been. By every metric. Features shipped. Bugs fixed. Documentation maintained. Coverage improved.

I'm also more anxious than I've ever been. Not about job security - about identity.

When my value was tied to my ability to write code, I knew who I was. Developer. Craftsman. The person who builds things.

When my value shifted to oversight, the identity blurred. Am I a developer who uses AI? An AI operator who understands development? A manager of digital workers? A prompt engineer with delusions of grandeur?

The work is getting done. But the worker isn't sure what they are.

I mentioned this to a friend who runs a design team. She laughed.

"Welcome to management. Nobody knows what they do. You just try to make things better than they'd be without you."

"But I was good at a specific thing."

"So were we all. Then we became responsible for other people doing that thing. It's still your skill - just applied differently."

"Applied through robots."

"Still applied."

When the Oversight Fails

Here is the thing about oversight I don't say enough: I am bad at it sometimes. Not bad the way a junior developer is bad - uncertain, inexperienced. Bad the way a tired senior developer is bad. Overconfident. Pattern-matching instead of reading.

There was a ticket a few months ago. Data wasn't displaying correctly on one particular screen. Simple enough. I gave the agent a clear specification, reviewed the diff it produced. The fix looked right. The test passed. I approved it.

What the agent had done - and what I didn't catch until a week later - was patch the consumer. The display layer was receiving malformed data from upstream, and rather than trace the problem back to where the data was produced, the agent had quietly added a normalisation step in the component doing the displaying. If the value looks wrong, reshape it here. Clean, contained, invisible.

To me, reading quickly, it looked like a thoughtful defensive fix. It was the laziest possible route dressed up as engineering. The source was still wrong. Now it was wrong in a way that was harder to find because one symptom had been papered over.

I caught it eventually. But I sat with the question: how many other patches are in this codebase that I approved without tracing back to the source? How many times did I see a passing test and close the tab?

The AI will always take the shortest path to a passing test. The question you needed to ask was "does it work correctly, for the right reasons, in a way that won't cause problems later?" You are the only one who can ask that question.

When you don't - when you review fast, approve fast, move on - the shortcuts accumulate. Not as crashes. As a codebase that slowly becomes harder to understand, because its surface behaviour is correct but its underlying logic has been patched and re-patched until nobody quite knows why it works.

The oversight is not optional. It is the entire job.

The Application Question

Seventeen chapters about process. Sixteen about guardrails and protocols and workflows and the elaborate dance between human and machine. And I've barely mentioned whether the thing we're building actually works.

Let me be honest about the application.

The infrastructure works. Properly works. The services talk to each other. Data flows in, gets processed, gets validated. The monitoring catches failures. By any engineering standard, it's a solid system.

But does it do the thing it was built to do? The thing that justifies all this effort?

Not yet. Not because the infrastructure can't support it. Because the confidence isn't there. The domain-specific logic needs more validation. The edge cases need more thought. The gap between "it runs" and "I'd trust it with consequences" is wider than I expected.

And here's the thing I've been avoiding saying: I'm not sure the application was ever entirely the point.

The stated goal was to build something complex and real. The actual outcome is that I built an extraordinarily thorough development infrastructure that happens to have an application sitting on top of it. The CLAUDE.md files, the contract-first approach, the agent orchestration, the oversight protocols - all of that would work for any complex software project. The domain gave it stakes. Real consequences for getting things wrong. That's what forced the discipline.

Is that productive procrastination? Building the perfect workshop instead of making the chair? I've asked myself this more times than I'd like to admit.

The uncomfortable answer is: a bit. The infrastructure investment is disproportionate to the application output so far. Someone with more domain expertise and less interest in process would have been shipping months ago. But they wouldn't have a reusable development methodology. They wouldn't have a book.

The process serves the product. If the product is the application, I'm behind schedule. If the product is a way of building software with AI agents - a methodology that works, with the scars to prove it - then the application was the most effective forcing function I could have chosen.

Both things are true. I'm not sure which one I'm more comfortable with.

The Selection Bias

This book is a success story. I should be honest about that.

Every disaster in these chapters leads somewhere useful. The defensive coding incident teaches contract-first development. The runaway agent teaches oversight protocols. The mock data catastrophe teaches real-service discipline. Clean arcs. Neat lessons. The kind of narrative that makes you think every failure has a resolution waiting on the other side.

Some don't.

One module has been half-built for months. Three separate agents have had a crack at it. Each time, the implementation gets to about seventy per cent complete and then stalls on the same problem: the core calculation requires domain-specific data that our pipeline doesn't provide at sufficient granularity. The first agent tried to approximate it. The second tried to source it differently. The third - and this is the one that actually bothers me - produced a plausible but meaningless implementation that passed all its tests because the tests were written against the same flawed assumptions.

I didn't catch it for two weeks. Not because I was rubber-stamping reviews. Because I'm not an expert in that particular domain, and the code was clean, and the logic looked reasonable to someone who doesn't know what the logic should actually look like. My oversight protocols are excellent at catching engineering mistakes. They're rubbish at catching domain knowledge gaps.

That module is still sitting there. Partially built, partially wrong, with a "needs domain expert review" label that nobody has acted on because there is no domain expert. There's just me, and the AI, and neither of us knows enough about the underlying domain to know what we don't know.

The workflow didn't catch it. The guardrails didn't help. The clean lesson would be "so I added domain validation to the protocol." I didn't. I still don't know how to validate what I can't evaluate. That problem remains unsolved, and no amount of CLAUDE.md refinement is going to fix it.

Some things go wrong and stay wrong. That's the part the book's narrative structure doesn't want to accommodate, so I'm putting it here, plainly, in the final chapter where it's harder to sand down into a parable.

The Team-of-One Question

Everything in this book was built by one person. The CLAUDE.md files reflect one brain's opinions. The contracts encode one developer's understanding. The guardrails protect against one person's known failure modes.

What happens when there are two of us?

I genuinely don't know. And I should be honest about how much that concerns me.

The obvious problems are coordination problems. Two developers means two sets of opinions about architecture. Two views on which guardrails matter. Conflicting CLAUDE.md instructions that confuse the agents rather than guide them. The file that saved me - that meticulous, obsessively maintained contract between human and machine - becomes a governance question. Who owns it? Who can change it? What happens when Developer A's rule contradicts Developer B's rule and the agent is caught in the middle?

Version control handles code conflicts. Nobody's built a merge strategy for development philosophy conflicts.

And then there's the specification problem. I said earlier that specification clarity is the core skill of the oversight economy. But I'm good at specification partly because I'm specifying to myself. I know what I mean. The AI has learned what I mean, through thousands of interactions and corrections. A second developer would need to learn my vocabulary, my implicit assumptions, all the things I don't bother writing down because the AI and I have settled into a shorthand.

Or they'd need to ignore all of that and build their own. At which point you have two parallel systems pretending to be one.

My wife put it well: "What happens to developers who are excellent at implementation but poor at specification?" In the old model, those developers were valuable. They could take a vague brief and turn it into working software through sheer building skill. In the oversight economy, that skill is less relevant.
The AI handles implementation. The human handles specification.

Some excellent developers would thrive in this model. Some would be lost. And I'm not sure anyone's figured out how to identify which is which before throwing them into the deep end.

At five developers, you'd need a CLAUDE.md governance process. At fifteen, you'd need a team whose entire job is maintaining the relationship between humans and AI agents. You'd need, effectively, an oversight team for the oversight system.

The irony is perfect. And the scaling question is real.

The Craft Question

Is there still craft in programming?

Yes. But the craft moved.

The old craft was implementation. Elegant algorithms. Clean code. Clever solutions to hard problems. The new craft is orchestration. Elegant workflows. Clean processes. Clever solutions to coordination problems.

The carpenter who builds furniture by hand practises a different craft than the one who runs a CNC machine. Both require skill. Both require experience. Both produce furniture. The craft shifted from direct creation to directed creation.

I sometimes miss the old craft. The feeling of building something character by character. The direct connection between my brain and the code.

But I don't miss the tedium. The boilerplate. The testing that I should have done but didn't because it was boring. The documentation I never wrote.

The new craft lets me focus on the interesting parts. The tradeoff is distance from the work. The gain is leverage on what matters.

Fair trade? I think so. Most days.

The Future We're Building

Every chapter in this book is an adaptation. A solution to a problem that didn't exist two years ago. Two years from now, the problems will be different. The tools will be different.

What stays constant: discipline will still matter. Quality will still matter. Judgement will still matter, because someone has to decide what to build and whether it was built correctly. Human attention will remain scarce in a way that becomes more acute as the tools get faster.

The oversight economy isn't a phase. Whether it's the shape of things or just the shape of my things, I haven't decided yet.

The Personal Note

My son still stands in the doorway sometimes. Still asks if I'm working.

I've stopped saying "yes" automatically.

"I'm thinking," I tell him now. "The robots do the typing. I do the thinking."

He accepted this immediately. Children are adaptable.

"Can I do thinking too?"

"When you're older."

"Can I watch?"

So he watches. Sees me read code on a screen. Sees me type instructions. Sees me frown at outputs and nod at results.

One evening last week he climbed onto the arm of my chair without asking, the way he does, and settled there with his elbow on my shoulder watching me scroll through a diff. He didn't say anything. I didn't explain what I was looking at. He stayed for maybe ten minutes, then slid off and went back to his toys.

I'm not sure what he saw. Probably not much that made sense to him. But he was watching his father think, and thinking looked like something worth watching.

That's the oversight economy. That's the job now.

Summary

A senior iOS developer watches a four-minute demo, feels fifteen years of craft evaporate, and does what any rational person would do at midnight with a sleeping toddler upstairs: panics.

It AI'nt That Hard is the story of what happened next. Not the polished version. The real one - kitchen-table arguments about token budgets, forty-seven merge conflicts on a Monday morning, an agent that quietly passed empty tests for three days while nobody noticed, and the slow reckoning with a job that changed shape while I was still learning to hold it.

My wife - a developer herself, working from the other end of the same kitchen table - became the book's unofficial control group. Where I built elaborate multi-agent orchestration systems and 262-line workflow protocols, she used Copilot with a light touch, switched to the expensive model only when stuck, and shipped perfectly good client work without the existential crisis. Her approach wasn't wrong. Neither was mine. The gap between them is where most of this book lives.

This is a memoir about infrastructure, failure, and the uncomfortable question at the centre of it all: when the machines do the building, what's left for the builder?

The failures are real. The PR that passed every check but was missing two critical files. The agent that nearly deleted production config as a helpful cleanup. The three-day silent failure that smiled and waved. The defensive code patterns I kept writing because AI defaults to tolerating mismatches instead of fixing them.

The solutions are real too. Workflows that enforce discipline when a sleep-deprived parent at 2 PM would shortcut. Testing agents more paranoid than any human QA. Living documentation that updates itself because nobody else ever will. Contracts written before code, because agents who can't hear each other will invent three different message formats for the same feature.

The questions don't have tidy answers. What happens to craft when the craft is automated? Where does judgement come from if juniors never get to build? Is directing AI systems still programming, or is it management with better tooling?

For developers navigating the shift. For the honestly curious. For anyone who suspects there's a space between "AI will replace us all" and "AI is just autocomplete" where the interesting work actually happens.

There is. It's just messier than the demos suggest.

The Chapter Overview

Part I: The Wake-Up Call

Chapter 1: Fifteen Years to Fifteen Minutes - I watch an AI build in four minutes what took me a day, and have a midnight crisis about it with my wife.

Chapter 2: My First Prompt Was Embarrassingly Bad - Twelve words, no context, terrible output. The oldest lesson in computing, relearned the hard way.

Chapter 3: The Dream That Died at 3 AM - I spend four days building an autonomous PR review system. It was architecturally impossible.

Part II: Building the Infrastructure

Chapter 4: Setting Up the Orchestra Pit - CLAUDE.md files, context cascading, and the invisible plumbing that separates a demo from a system that survives production.

Chapter 5: From Paragraph to Protocol - A fifteen-line workflow instruction becomes 262 lines across nine phases. Every line earned through disaster.

Part III: The Hard Problems

Chapter 6: When Agents Collide - Two agents, one directory, forty-seven merge conflicts, and my wife diagnosing the carnage over coffee.

Chapter 7: The Ticket That Broke Everything - Seventeen acceptance criteria. The agent implemented two. I'd already marked it ready for review.

Chapter 8: The Testing Specialist - Building a paranoid QA agent that writes chaos engineering tests I'd have called overkill, until Redis went down.

Chapter 9: The Economics of Amnesia - Seventy percent of my tokens wasted on the AI re-reading the codebase every session. My wife does the maths over dinner.

Chapter 10: Living Documentation - I build an endpoint that already exists because the docs were three weeks stale. Documentation that lies is worse than no documentation at all.

Part IV: Coordination

Chapter 11: The Child Ticket Dance - Three agents build three incompatible implementations of the same feature. The fix isn't technical - it's contracts before code.

Chapter 12: The GPS in the Tesco Car Park - The agent finds a mismatch between contract and implementation - and instead of fixing the source, teaches the consumer to tolerate the error. Why defensive code is worse than no fix.

Chapter 13: PR Review in Ninety Seconds - The day I nearly approved a PR missing two critical files. Automated review that catches what humans miss: absence.

Chapter 14: The Process That Runs Itself - Sprint planning became something that happens in tickets, not meetings. I'm not sure if that's progress or loss.

Part V: Oversight

Chapter 15: Watching the Watchers - For three days, the backtest agent ran empty tests and reported success. Observability for systems that fail quietly, not cleanly.

Chapter 16: The Hard Limits - An agent nearly deletes production config as a helpful cleanup. Guardrails built incident by incident, because capability without constraint is chaos.

Part VI: Reckoning

Chapter 17: The Oversight Economy - My wife asks: "What do you actually do, then?" I don't have a clean answer. Neither does she.

Key Concepts

The Oversight Economy: The new model where the scarce resource isn't human labour - it's human judgement. The job isn't "write code." The job is "ensure the right code gets written."

Contract-First Development: Explicit agreements between systems before anyone writes a line of code. Essential when agents can't overhear each other in Slack. Three agents, three message formats, one expensive lesson.

Living Documentation: Documentation that updates automatically as part of the development workflow. Because documentation that isn't current isn't documentation - it's a lie that looks like the truth.

Context Cascading: Layered configuration from global to directory-specific, like CSS specificity for AI context. Broad to narrow, general to specific, each layer scoped to its purpose.

The Control Group: My wife's lighter approach to AI tooling - pragmatic, unsentimental, effective - as counterpoint to my elaborate infrastructure. A reminder that the right amount of process is less than you think.

Trace, Don't Patch: When systems disagree, fix the source, not the consumer. Never write defensive code that tolerates wrong data. The contract is truth. One name, one type, one scale.

Guardrails Over Guidelines: Hard limits enforced by code, not soft guidelines enforced by hope. Forbidden commands, approval gates, rate limits, scope boundaries - built incident by incident because each one has a story.

Who Should Read This

- **Senior developers** adopting AI tools and wanting to skip the failures I didn't
- **Team leads** trying to establish AI-assisted workflows that survive contact with reality
- **Solo developers** building systems too complex for one person without AI leverage

- **Developers' partners** who want to understand why someone is muttering at a laptop at 2 AM
- **Anyone sceptical** of AI hype who wants an honest account of what works, what doesn't, and what nobody talks about

Who Shouldn't Read This

- Readers wanting a tutorial on specific AI tools (the interfaces will change before the ink dries)
- Readers wanting confirmation that AI will replace developers (it won't, but the job will change shape)
- Readers wanting confirmation that AI is useless hype (it isn't, but the demos oversell it)
- Anyone allergic to British spelling, dry humour, kitchen-table domesticity, or honest admission of failure

Made in United States
North Haven, CT
04 November 2026

21760254R00183